Remember the
"Good Life" in Lincoln
Marie Hirst

Remember the
"Good Life" in Lincoln
Marie Hirst

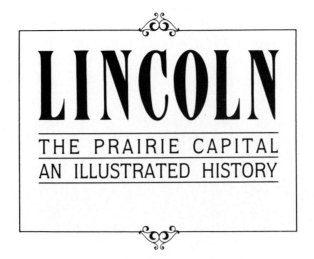

LINCOLN

THE PRAIRIE CAPITAL
AN ILLUSTRATED HISTORY

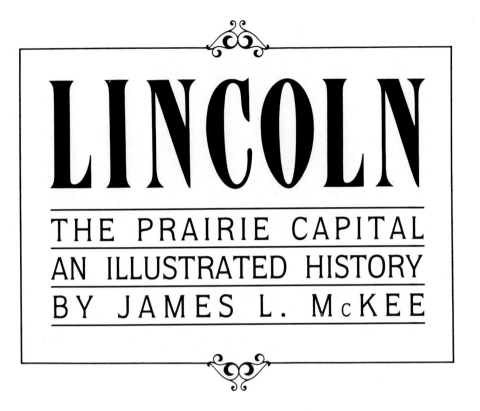

LINCOLN

THE PRAIRIE CAPITAL
AN ILLUSTRATED HISTORY
BY JAMES L. McKEE

PICTURE RESEARCH BY JOHN G. GOECKE
"PARTNERS IN PROGRESS" BY JACK L. KENNEDY

PRODUCED IN COOPERATION WITH THE
LINCOLN-LANCASTER COUNTY HISTORICAL SOCIETY

WINDSOR PUBLICATIONS, INC.
WOODLAND HILLS, CALIFORNIA

Page two: The mosaic in the north vestibule dome of the capitol represents the gifts of nature to man, with a "sun" surrounded by panels that illustrate the fruits of the soil.

Windsor Publications
History Books Division
Publisher: John M. Phillips
Senior Picture Editor: Teri Davis Greenberg
Editorial Director, Corporate Biographies: Karen Story
Assistant Director, Corporate Biographies: Phyllis Gray
Marketing Director: Ellen Kettenbeil
Sales Coordinator: Joan Baker
Design Director: Alexander D'Anca

Staff for *Lincoln: The Prairie Capital*
Editors: Annette Igra, Margaret Tropp, Sarah Tringali
Picture Editor: Laurel H. Paley
Corporate Biographies Editor: Judith Hunter
Editorial Assistants: Kathy M. Brown, Patricia Buzard, Gail Koffman, Lonnie Pham,
  Pat Pittman
Sales Manager: Ernie Fredette
Sales Representative: Clive Bates
Layout Artist: Lisa Robertson

Library of Congress Cataloguing in Publication Data

McKee, James L.
    Lincoln, the prairie capital.

    "Produced in cooperation with the Lincoln-Lancaster County Historical Society."
    Bibliography: p. 187
    Includes index.
    1. Lincoln (Neb.)—History. 2. Lincoln (Neb.)—Description. 3. Lincoln (Neb.)—Industries. I. Title.
F674.L7M33   1984   978.2'293   84-20796
ISBN 0-89781-109-7

CONTENTS

PREFACE

Historically, cities have usually been founded on navigable waterways, or at fords, or at places where trade routes crossed. The site of Lincoln, Nebraska, had no such preexisting assets. It became, like the later cities of Canberra and Brasilia, a capital before it was even a sizable village. It was on a small saline stream (referred to by early prairie optimists as a river), which was joined within a few miles by half a dozen smaller streams; none of these could float even a canoe. The nearest "trade route" was the Oregon Trail Cutoff, eight miles to the south. It did have one singular asset: a seasonal salt flat that served the Indians and became a focus for migrants and settlers. When the railroads came, they followed the streams, so this shallow meeting place of watercourses became the center of a spiderweb of rail lines radiating literally in all directions.

When the Nebraska Territory became a state, a commission was appointed to find a site for a capital, well inland from the older towns along the Missouri River. This was not a particularly promising spot: on the very eastern edge of what was then known as the Great American Desert, at the western edge of known cultivable land. Pioneer optimism, aided by political rivalries—not between other towns, but between two major geographical areas—thus brought to life this isolated pinpoint on the prairie. It had no real or potential industry (the salt business proved unprofitable), and it lacked firewood, building stone, and surface water. But for an economic foundation it had the state and county offices, the state university, the penitentiary, and a state hospital.

For its first few years, Lincoln, at the end of a westbound railway line, became the jumping-off point for settlers bound farther west, and thus also became their major supply point. As other railroads came in, it became a division point for four of the five roads, thus gaining a permanent artisan population to add to the government workers and the increasing numbers of buyers and sellers. And from then on, it grew.

Early pictures show the town as consisting of a few dozen houses and buildings scattered almost randomly about on a bare, treeless prairie. Except for trees along watercourses, and farm windbreaks, the outlying countryside still looks like open prairie, even though now richly farmed. But Lincoln, almost in the middle of the United States, has a "continental climate"—which means that in summer hot winds blow constantly all the way from Texas, and in winter very cold winds come down from Manitoba. This climate, plus the encouragement of J. Sterling Morton, father of Arbor Day, prompted the copious planting of trees. For some 50 years one of my pleasures has been taking visitors from the wooded East to the observation deck of the Capitol and saying, "Look out there," at the prairie, and then, "Now look down"—into a sea of trees interrupted only by a few church spires. Except for the downtown and industrial areas, and the newest subdivisions, the scene looks—well, almost—like a forest. And when I point out that all those trees have been, at one time and another, hand-planted, the visitors are impressed. And, frankly, so am I.

This book is the story of the prairie capital's growth from a tiny settlement on the edge of a salt flat to a thriving modern city. I know of no one better fitted than James McKee, a longtime student of local history, to try to set down that story.

Wilbur Gaffney
Professor Emeritus,
University of Nebraska

In June 1869 the Capital Commission members were joined by Mr. Thielson of the Burlington and Missouri River Railroad in breaking ground near the site of the pictured depot west of P Street. Although a small wooden structure served temporarily as a depot at about 7th and S streets, this three-story brick building was built in 1870 as the first real railroad depot in the city. The building was replaced in 1925 by a new brick and stone structure designed to handle the passengers of both the Union Pacific and the Burlington railroads.

7

CHAPTER

▮

INDIANS AND EXPLORERS

The Pawnee was the largest Indian tribe in Nebraska before the region became a territory, and virtually the only group to reside in Lancaster County. Numbering nearly 10,000 at the time of the Louisiana Purchase, the Pawnee's population was reduced to 649 by 1906. Omaha photographer William Henry Jackson captured a group of four Pawnee scouts about 1869.

In 1536 four starving and half-crazed men stumbled into Mexico City with a tale that was to send the first explorers into the Kansas-Nebraska area. They were said to be the sole survivors of nearly 400 Spanish troops landed eight years earlier on the coast of Florida. During their wanderings, they traveled in an arc that reached north to what would be the Kansas-Nebraska border and then south into Mexico. Their tales of cities paved with gold, where even the lowliest ate and cooked with silver and gold vessels, gave rise to the often-expanded legend of Quivera. Almost at once an expedition to weigh the possibilities of colonization was dispatched under the direction of Marcos de Niza, who returned with even more stories of the Seven Cities of Cibola. These stories were concocted by the leader in order to return home as quickly as possible and with as much honor as could be salvaged. The immediate result was an even greater expedition headed by Francisco Vásquez de Coronado.

In early 1541 Coronado's party set out. As they traveled, they "Christianized" by looting, capturing, burning, and generally terrorizing the Indians in their path. One native known as Yspete, intent on moving the Spanish out of his village, told new and even more dazzling stories of Quivera to the northeast, where there was a river seven miles wide. Within its depths were huge fish as large as horses. Tartarrax, the ruler, slept in a garden of roses under a tree with thousands of golden bells, and even the pots and pans were made of

silver and gold. Coronado hastened north and east, with his guide spurring him onward at every junction. In this manner they covered nearly 800 miles and reached the Arkansas River. From there they were led and directed north, though Coronado became more and more suspicious. When they found the promised wide water, they supposed they had discovered Quivera, but they saw no gold, silver, roses, or tinkling bells. Though Coronado claimed he had discovered Quivera and reported that the land was "fat and black...the best I have ever seen," he promptly hanged the guide. Nebraska had now been officially discovered by the white man. The discovery of Spanish horse trappings near the Republican River in the 1890s marked that as the probable site of Coronado's Quivera.

Beginning in 1606 the British government generously awarded the Plymouth and Massachusetts Bay companies land grants that stretched to the Pacific Ocean. This area hardly constituted a crown possession, however, and no exploration traversed the region. The Great Northwest Territory was claimed by Spain in 1673, by France in 1683, by Spain again in 1762, and once again by France in 1800. Because Napoleon feared he might ultimately lose the territory to the British, he promptly sold the nearly one million square miles bounded by the Mississippi River, the Rocky Mountains, the Gulf of Mexico, and British America for $15 million—or about 2.6 cents per acre—in 1803. The following year President Thomas Jefferson sought to

Peter Sarpy, as representative of the American Fur Company, was an early Nebraska pioneer and one of the settlers of Bellevue. Sarpy County was named in his honor.

After the Louisiana Purchase of 1803, many expeditions followed Meriwether Lewis and William Clark into the region. Major Stephen H. Long, pictured, was one of the first to refer on a map to the area west of Lancaster County as the "Great American Desert."

protect the purchase by planting the American flag, determining what natural resources were available, and charting a passage to the Pacific. To this end the Lewis and Clark Expedition was formed. In July 1804 the party camped on the Little Nemaha River, and ownership of Nebraska's portion of the United States was reaffirmed by right of discovery.

Although fur traders had established "posts" in the 18th century, popular legend has it that Colonel Peter Sarpy made the first permanent settlement in Nebraska for the American Fur Company in 1810 at Bellevue. Most historians agree that Bellevue's claim predates others, though the date of 1823 is often preferred. Hard on the heels of the first explorers came the missionaries, eager to establish contact with the natives. Bellevue was also chosen as a locale for a mission by the Baptist Church, which sent the Reverend Moses P. Merrill who, with his wife, established a school in 1833. Pathfinders such as John C. Frémont, the Mormon emigrants, and mapmakers with Stephen Long's Yellowstone Expedition were soon traversing the "District Louisiana." The "Great American Desert," which stretched from the Platte Valley to the Red River, was thus charted and generally considered uninhabitable. The area that was to become Lancaster County formed the eastern edge of this formidable tract of land.

Beginning with the Thomas Fitzpatrick party in 1841, a trail was blazed and later reinforced by general emigration and the Great Pathfinder, John C. Frémont. Like the Santa Fe Trail, it began at Independence, Missouri. Forty miles from the trailhead a sign announced the northward turn for the "Road to Oregon." Although this road missed Lancaster County, a connection called the Oregon Trail Cutoff was greatly to influence the settlements in its path and would later play a part in the capital selection.

Although the Indians played a major role in the problems and development of the Territory of Nebraska, in the area of Lancaster County the Indians offered only occasional resistance to settlement. Other

than camps, only two archeologically
significant Indian sites have been found;
apparently only the nomadic Pawnee were
ever present for any period of time. South
of the Cadman Stage Station at Salt Creek
and Saltillo Road, a 15-acre village site
dating from A.D. 1000 to 1500 has been
recorded. Near 11th and High streets in
Lincoln is the site of a reported, though
unconfirmed, Pawnee council site. This is
said to have been a trial ground for chiefs
and important officials because of the high
ground. A defendant found guilty would
then be buried in an appropriate low area.
Here, too, is the abandoned Robbers' Cave
or Pawnee council cave, where part of the
white community is said to have hidden
during an 1862 Indian scare.

Lancaster County's first permanent
settler, John W. Prey, arrived in June 1856.
Within a few months a handful of
pioneers, probably less than a dozen, were
in residence. The threat of Indian attack
was constantly in the settlers' minds, but
their first year passed without incident. As
corn-planting time arrived in the spring of
1857, a few newcomers showed up. Chief
among them in vocal prowess was a man
named Davis. Mr. Davis vowed to shoot
himself an Indian, which on his first, albeit
unprovoked, opportunity he did. Virtually
the only Indians in the entire county were
nomadic Omaha, Pawnee, and Otoe, who
were far from warlike. They did have a
penchant for harassing the timid and were
always on the lookout for coffee and food.
Though peaceful, they were considerably
put out by the murder and began
gathering in numbers, which caused the
settlers to sound the alarm and head for
the closest town of consequence, Weeping
Water, 40 miles northeast. There they
remained for two weeks, sending occasional
scouting parties to see if the coast was
clear. Meantime a force of nearly 100 was
dispatched from Nebraska City to put
down the uprising. After capturing a lone
Pawnee, they saw no more Indians, and the
party returned to Nebraska City. A few
hours after his capture, the brave asked to
step outside and was last seen running off
in the distance. The settlers returned to

*Pawnee Chief
Peta-la-sha-ra was
photographed by William
Henry Jackson in 1868.*

Above: A photograph was made in 1961 of this frame building, all that remained of Moses and Eliza Merrill's Baptist missionary school, built in Bellevue in 1833.

Opposite: This 1853 sketch by Frederick Piercy shows the Council Bluffs Ferry, which connected Iowa with the western banks of the Missouri. The ferry operated before Nebraska became an official territory.

their much-delayed planting. Like the Indian, Mr. Davis was not seen again.

Other minor scares cropped up from time to time with no reportable result. In 1864, on word of a Sioux uprising, the women, children, and many of the men again left their claims, leaving a few behind to keep watch. Among these was John Prey who, with a few of the others, decided to ride west a bit to see if there really was any danger. All they encountered was a band of several hundred Pawnee, who scared them badly but announced that they, too, were on the lookout for the Sioux.

Early efforts in 1844 and 1851 to establish a territory west of Iowa and Missouri ran up against the question of whether the territory would be free or slave, as well as unanswered problems surrounding the government treaties establishing the land west of the Missouri River as permanent Indian territory. A similar bill in 1852, which would have created the Platte Territory out of the present Kansas area north to the Platte

River, likewise failed. The establishment of territories was greatly favored by Iowans, who had their eyes on the vast unowned lands across the river, which would not be open for development until an official territory was created. On a fresh proposal by Senator Stephen A. Douglas, the Kansas-Nebraska Act passed Congress on May 30, 1854. Although the size and shape of Kansas is relatively unchanged today, the Nebraska Territory included all of the present state plus the Dakotas, Colorado up to the Rocky Mountains, and much of Wyoming, Montana, and Idaho. The resulting 351,588-square-mile territory was immediately opened for settlement except for several areas set aside as Indian reservations. It is interesting to note that the Republican party, which had as its foremost plank a "no slave" proposal, was born at the same time.

Each original Nebraska settlement had a corresponding champion on the Iowa side of the river. Residents of Bluff City, later Council Bluffs, extolled the virtues of Omaha City, hoping to establish their own

city as a terminus of an imminent western railroad. The Council Bluffs and Nebraska Ferry Company was quickly formed and soon held land in Nebraska. James Mitchell, also of Council Bluffs, had the site of the old Mormon winter quarters in mind for a city that would become Florence. The *Nebraska Palladian,* though printed in Iowa, boosted Bellevue as a natural site for the territorial capital.

Having officially granted territorial status to Nebraska, President Franklin Pierce asked William Butler to accept an appointment as governor. When Butler declined, Francis Burt of Pendleton, South Carolina, was chosen. Burt was an excellent choice, having been an attorney, editor, state treasurer, legislator, and third auditor of the U.S. Treasury. Burt received his commission August 2, 1854, and set out with his son for Nebraska on September 11. The pair traveled by horse and buggy, railroad, stagecoach, riverboat, wagon, and hack, so it was no wonder that Burt was forced to rest a few days in St. Louis before continuing his trek to Nebraska. He arrived in Bellevue, which was virtually the only spot in the territory that could be even loosely referred to as a city, on October 7. He planned to rest a few days at Father Hamilton's Presbyterian mission house and then seek out a good local spot to build a capitol. On October 16 he took the oath of office from his bed, and there he died on October 18, having never risen. There was little doubt in the minds of his son and several others who visited him that Burt intended Bellevue to be the capital, but this fact was never officially recorded.

As there was no provision for a lieutenant governor, the secretary of the territory, Thomas B. Cuming of Keokuk, Iowa, became acting governor. Using the very bedroom where Father Hamilton was readying Burt's body for transport by sealing it in a metal coffin, Cuming instructed Judge Barton Green, Burt's son Armistead, and several of the men who had arrived with Burt to return the body to South Carolina. Judge Green was to leave the rest of the party before reaching

Above: Located on the west side of 9th Street between Douglas and Farnam streets in Omaha, the first territorial capitol served the first legislature, which convened in January 1855. The building was built by the Council Bluffs & Nebraska Ferry Company at a cost of $3,000.

Opposite: Nebraska's second territorial capitol stood on the present site of Omaha Central High School, at the top of Capitol Avenue. The $100,000 cost of the building was shared by the federal government and the City of Omaha.

South Carolina and proceed to New York in hopes of raising $50,000, the asking price for the mission property that would become the basis for the capital. The money was not forthcoming, and Cuming asked Father Hamilton to deed the mission property to him; in exchange he would guarantee the capital for Bellevue. Hamilton countered that he would give it to the county or territory but not directly to Cuming.

It now appears that Cuming, having received several offers regarding the capital, realized that a great deal of political power if not personal wealth hung in the balance. Cuming not only owed his very office to political powers in Iowa, but also he actually resided in Council Bluffs, though he listed his residence as Omaha. The Iowa interests, seeing great benefit for Council Bluffs, began pushing for Omaha as the capital of Nebraska, citing its favorable location. The governor was required by the U.S. territorial directive to set political

boundaries in the form of legislative districts and call for a territorial census. The former task was performed easily by establishing eight counties. The latter was considerably more difficult, as the Kansas-Nebraska border was not defined and many of the "residents" had come over from Iowa only for the purpose of being counted. On November 20, 1854, the census was completed and showed a total population of 2,732.

The territory was instantly divided into those who lived north of the Platte, where Omaha was located, and those to the south. The South Platte population was 1,818, almost twice the population of the North Platters, at 914. This would ordinarily have meant that legislative power would go to the south. Cuming, however, gave the north seven seats in the Council and 14 in the House of Representatives, while the south received only six seats in the Council and 12 in the House. At a meeting to argue this division,

Governor Cuming said that he had uncovered an error in the census which now gave the north a greater population and that in addition the north was growing faster. He was also quoted as saying that if Bellevue would nominate one person for the Council and two for the House who would vote with him in the capital selection, he would create a separate district for Bellevue. Almost at once the South Platte area was the scene of numerous meetings seeking Cuming's removal from office. On December 20, 1854, Cuming at last made official what the South Platters knew would ultimately happen and announced that the territorial legislature would meet at Omaha.

At 10 a.m. on January 16, 1855, the first territorial legislature convened in the building owned by the Council Bluffs and Nebraska Ferry Company, a firm partially owned by Acting Governor Cuming. The furnishings were all secondhand, with most of the legislators sharing two-person school desks and tables. After much squabbling over the credentials of virtually every member, Omaha was officially labeled the capital.

On February 20 the President appointed Mark W. Izard of Kentucky the territory's second governor. One of his first acts was to suggest that the civil code of Iowa be virtually rubber-stamped for use in Nebraska. Most of the legislators, being from Iowa or at least in sympathy with it,

agreed that this was a good idea and so acted. After about half of Izard's term had expired, he left the territory for Washington, hoping to resign and have the President appoint a new governor. William A. Richardson of Illinois was appointed in May 1857, but he declined. Izard returned to Nebraska under constant fire for his lack of leadership, and ultimately he did resign in October. Secretary Cuming again acted as governor till Richardson formally

Above: As this illustration shows, arguments in the territorial legislature were often spirited affairs, with many debates punctuated by the sounds of smashing chairs and an occasional gunshot.

Left: After Governor Francis Burt died—two days after he was sworn in—the position of governor was filled by Secretary Thomas Cuming until Mark W. Izard was appointed in 1855. Izard, pictured, was considered "the very quintessence of ignorance, indolence, and imbecility" by the editors of the Florence Courier. His resignation in 1857 again gave the office of governor, temporarily, to Thomas Cuming.

accepted. The city of Omaha had now raised $52,000 by a great scheme of printing its own money and with it supplemented federal funds to construct a proper capitol at the crest of Capitol Avenue. This plan, Omahans believed, would ensure their retaining the seat of government, though each session was full of contenders attempting to win it.

In 1859 the usual bill for capital removal was broached by legislator Joshua Abbe of Otoe County. The claim now current was that the $50,000 allowed by the federal government was expended, $52,000 of Omaha funds had been exhausted, an additional territorial obligation of $8,000 had been issued, and still the capitol was unfinished. Omaha legislators promised that if the removal bill passed, they would so foul up the wheels of government that no further legislation of any kind would be allowed to pass during the session. Those who favored removal pointed out that Omaha really had not given the territory anything. Legally Omaha had a claim to the land the building was standing on and a $52,000 lien on the building itself. The mayor of Omaha acted quickly to quash this claim by releasing the land and all interest in the building, but it was too late. A majority of both houses voted to withdraw from Omaha and reconvene at Florence, where the removal bill passed. The act provided a location and even stated that the name of the new capital would be Neapolis. Governor Richardson, however, refused to sign any of the bills drawn at Florence, with the net result that nearly an entire legislative session had been frittered away. The details read like a Gilbert and Sullivan operetta that would not ordinarily be believed by any but the most gullible observer.

The South Platters were not about to forget their previous losses and fought in every way they could think of to wrest the capital from Omaha. What may have begun as mere harassment of the North Platters once again came to a head in January 1856, when J. Sterling Morton petitioned the U.S. Senate and House of Representatives to withdraw that portion of Nebraska south of the Platte River and annex it to Kansas. Unfortunately—or fortunately, depending on one's point of view—Kansas was, for the most part, uninterested in or downright negative to the proffered expansion. This led briefly to talk of a separate state to exist between Kansas and the Platte River.

The secession question finally quieted, and for a time the territory concerned itself with the more mundane and now somewhat repetitious question of capital removal, the growing question of statehood, and territorial reapportionment, as the south fell further and further behind the north in representation. On March 5, 1860, an election was held to test the citizens' feelings on statehood. The vote came out 2,372 against the move and 2,094 in favor. Arguments centered on the questions of slave versus free status and whether taxation would increase under statehood, as many of the territorial expenses were covered by the federal government. Nonetheless, the ninth legislature passed a joint resolution asking the U.S. Congress to pass an enabling act so that a state constitution could be drawn up preliminary to application for statehood. Congress complied, but so near the end of the session that little else could be done at that time.

By the 11th territorial session it was obvious that statehood was imminent. J. Sterling Morton was the most notable and vocal dissenter. Many Nebraskans considered the constitution thus drawn to have been forced down their throats, and it was the subject of vituperative debate, primarily about the Negro suffrage clause. Because of the restriction allowing the vote only to whites, Congress rejected the constitution. Nebraska's legislature was quickly called into special session on February 20, 1867, and by striking the words "free white" from the election law, redefined white as any color whatsoever. President Johnson, unimpressed by this tomfoolery, vetoed the bill. It was promptly passed over his veto, forcing him to frame the proclamation of March 1, 1867, that officially made Nebraska the 37th state.

CHAPTER ▌▌

VILLAGE BY THE SALT FLATS

The earliest permanent settler in Lancaster County was undoubtedly John W. Prey, who arrived in the spring of 1856. John Dee, who arrived shortly afterward and settled near Waverly, is often also mentioned as a serious contender for the honor. John D. Prey and his son John W. had started west from Milwaukee, intending to settle at Council Bluffs, Iowa. When they arrived there, they fell in with Zebediah Buffington, who pointed out that Iowa was already crowded. He convinced them to join him in crossing over into Nebraska to the Elkhorn Valley, which they also found too populous for their tastes. They then set off for Salt Creek, which reportedly boasted a large stand of timber and few if any settlers.

The Preys arrived near the salt basins on June 15, 1856, and met three men who, along with several others, had staked claims nearby but apparently had no intention of actually settling. At any rate, the county had not even been surveyed, and their claims were unrecorded for the time being. John W. Prey immediately set about the business of surveying the area and erecting a shelter, while his father returned to Pennsylvania to bring the rest of the family. The Preys staked five claims in Centerville Precinct, southwest of Lincoln, in what was then Clay County, an area not joined to Lancaster until 1864. Mr. Buffington filed a claim south of Roca but stayed only a short time before abandoning it. The Prey families arrived in late July and set up temporary shelter while starting work on log cabins. They brought a large

supply of provisions from Nebraska City in preparation for the coming winter, which proved to be the most severe recorded for many years, with snow depth at four feet on the level. In the spring the Preys found that many of their less hardy neighbors had given up during the winter and returned east. Their first crop of corn was small but encouraging, and subsequent harvests proved well up to their expectations.

By 1859 enough population was on hand to consider the official organization of a county. To this end a meeting of all settlers was called at the "Great Elm," about where S Street in Lincoln would now meet Salt Creek. The area they proposed incorporating was an extension of Cass County that had been tacked onto the existing county for political reasons, awaiting sufficient numbers of landowners to actually break off. An impromptu election was held, and Festus Reed was elected chairman. Mr. Reed appointed Joseph J. Forest and W.T. Donovan as a committee to determine the site of a county seat, which was given the name Lancaster after the county (named for Donovan's home town of Lancaster, Pennsylvania). Shortly afterward, on October 10, 1859, Cass County officials called for an election in the newly proposed county. This was held at the home of William Shirley, who lived on Stevens Creek. County officers were elected, and the group adjourned. The first official general election was held at the Donovan cabin, about a block and a half

This photo of Salt Creek shows the stream near Willow Bend—one of the few areas close to Lincoln where there were any trees—a popular swimming and fishing site.

Russell, Majors, and Waddell was the federal government's primary freighter along the Oregon Trail Cutoff as it passed through Lancaster County south of Lincoln. Pictured is Augustus A. Tylee, a wagon boss for Russell, Majors, and Waddell.

northeast of the present Burlington Station, at which 23 votes were cast. Little of consequence occurred until 1863, when J.S. Gregory was elected to the legislature from Lancaster County and John Cadman from Clay County to the south.

John Cadman originally came to the area in 1859 with a party of men he was escorting to the western goldfields. At Clay County they encountered a band returning from the goldfields carrying tales of woe. They took a vote and decided to go no farther, but to settle in Lancaster and Clay counties instead. Mr. Cadman took a claim on Salt Creek, which ultimately became the site of the village of Saltillo. This proved an ideal location, becoming the official ford for the Oregon Trail Cutoff. This major route was in fact the most heavily traveled portion of the Oregon Trail, though it was looked upon by emigrants as a minor connection from Nebraska City to Fort Kearny. An earlier route, called the Ox-Bow Trail, had wandered from Nebraska City to Ashland and thence to Fort Kearny. Residents of Nebraska City were quick to see that their major trail head could easily lose out to Omaha as an outfitting and river-crossing site. To prevent this they planned a more direct route, cutting just over 40 miles off the trip. This trail was initiated by a breaking plow whose driver left Nebraska City with instructions simply to find the best route to Fort Kearny. The first wagons then merely straddled the rut until a road was ultimately formed.

Within a short time the principal government freighters, Russell, Majors, and Waddell, had established Nebraska City as a freighting headquarters for all the government outposts and forts to the west. To this end they maintained a herd of 30,000 oxen and a supply of some 6,000 to 8,000 empty wagons. Many hundreds of wagons from Nebraska City simply carried a few extra rocks which they deposited in the Salt Creek and on both banks in order to build a stone passage in the mud that made the crossing unusable when the creek rose. So heavily traveled was this ford that up to six lanes of wagons converged at the crossing to wait their turn.

It was at this point that John Cadman established a stage station. He soon became well known in the area and was elected to the territorial legislature, but he was already becoming known not only for his hard work and political savvy but also for his practical jokes, which reportedly backfired as often as they succeeded.

Mr. Cadman proposed to John Gregory of Lancaster that they join forces to dissolve Clay County, giving the lower half to Gage County and the upper or northern half to Lancaster County. In return for his support Mr. Gregory was to be unopposed as postmaster of a village to be called Gregory's Basin, preserving his name on the area forever as well as giving him a federally salaried job. Mr. Cadman wanted the county seat for the village of Yankee Hill, which he had just platted northwest of Saltillo. Meantime John Gregory had convinced the legislature to appropriate $500 to build a bridge over Salt Creek. Mr. Cadman saw the obvious bridge site near Yankee Hill, while Mr. Gregory felt that his village was a more logical location. The resulting compromise gave each site $250, which had to be supplemented locally before any bridge could be built in either area.

Now the citizens of Clay County had to be convinced that it would be to their advantage to have Clay County disappear forever. To this end Mr. Cadman assured the citizens of Olathe (a settlement midway between Saltillo and Roca), Saltillo, and Yankee Hill that each would have the county seat. As each group thought that it had the county seat in the bag, the dissolution question passed easily. Just about that time, however, they discovered that Cadman intended the prize for himself. In 1864 they got their revenge by joining together in voting the county seat to Lancaster, recently renamed from the short-lived Gregory's Basin. John W. Prey, Clay County treasurer, ordered copies of the division sent up from the Gage County courthouse in Beatrice. To this end he deputized William Mills to bring back the books along with some flour he was

As Russell, Majors, and Waddell—later the instigator of the Pony Express—began its freight operation in Nebraska City, it advertised for men and oxen. The company maintained a constant herd of nearly 30,000 oxen to provide motive power for its freight wagon trains.

picking up. On his return Mills encountered a thunderstorm. Ill-advisedly, he sought to recross Salt Creek at the same spot he had used in going to Beatrice. Unfortunately the wagon capsized, losing the records, the flour, and very nearly Mr. Mills' life. The result was that the records never did arrive at the Lancaster County courthouse.

Indian legend gives us the earliest inkling of the salt flats northwest of the present city of Lincoln. They were first mentioned by John T. Irving, Jr., in his book *Indian Sketches, Taken During an Expedition to the Pawnee Tribes,* published in 1835. After a general introduction about his visit to the valley of the Saline River, or Salt Creek as we know it, Irving related the "Legend of the Saline River."

"Many years since," he began, "long before the whites had extended their march beyond the banks of the Mississippi River, a tribe of Indians resided upon the Platte." Among these was a warrior noted for his fierce and merciless disposition. He and his warriors forever plotted destruction to their enemies. Often he would steal off alone, to add new victims to the countless already slain. As fearful as he was to his enemies, he was equally dreaded by his own people. Only the daughter of the chief loved him.

Though she had many other admirers, she became his wife. Their mutual love was unbounded, but their happiness soon ended with her death. He quietly buried her and left the village, covered with war paint. After a month he returned with scalps of men, women, and children of his enemies and a large rock of white salt. After traveling many miles over the prairie, he said, he had camped as the moon was rising.

He started up, and at a little distance, by the light of the moon, beheld an old, decrepit hag, brandishing a tomahawk over the head of a young female, who was kneeling, imploring mercy. He approached them, but they seemed unconscious of his presence. The young female, finding her prayers unheeded, sprang and made a

desperate attempt to get possession of the tomahawk. A furious struggle ensued, but the old woman was victorious. Twisting one hand in the long black hair of her victim, she raised the weapon in her other and prepared to strike. The face of the young female was turned to the light, and the warrior beheld with horror the features of his deceased wife. In an instant he sprang forward, and his tomahawk was buried in the skull of the old squaw. But ere he had time to clasp the form of his wife, the ground opened, both sank from his sight, and on the spot appeared a rock of white salt. He had broken a piece from it and brought it to his tribe.

This tradition is still current among the different tribes of Indians frequenting that portion of the county. They also imagine that the rock is still under the custody of the old squaw, and that the only way to obtain a portion of it is to attack her. For this reason, before attempting to collect salt, they beat the ground with clubs and tomahawks, and each blow is considered as

Above: It was hoped that the salt works of Lincoln would provide a sound industrial base for the capital city. Brine was evaporated by the sun in large covered wooden vats on the dry lake bed. The salt works was photographed circa 1870.

Opposite: In 1856 Captain William T. Donovan arrived at the Gregory's Basin salt flats as a representative of the Crescent Salt Company of Plattsmouth. The Capital Commission chose his two-story cabin, which was about a block and a half northeast of the present Burlington station, as the site for its deliberations.

J. Sterling Morton, who was very nearly elected Nebraska's first state governor, obtained land patents for the area including Lincoln's salt flats. The secretary of the interior revoked the transactions, however, as saline lands were not subject to sale. In 1872 Morton made a motion to the Nebraska Board of Agriculture designating April 10 Arbor Day, a day of tree planting. Governor Furnas proclaimed it a state holiday and moved it to April 22, Morton's birthday. National recognition followed in 1885.

inflicted upon the person of the hag. The ceremony is continued until they imagine she has been sufficiently belabored to resign her treasure without opposition.

Because of the salt flats the federal government, in 1856, ordered a land survey of the area and its surroundings. The results of the survey were to make the area instantly attractive to settlement and industrial development because of the scarcity and resulting high price of salt. Captain W.T. Donovan, representing the Crescent Salt Company of Plattsmouth, was probably the first serious salt hunter, settling on the west bank of Salt Creek near the Oak Creek intersection in 1856. He named his claim Lancaster after his home in Pennsylvania. Donovan was soon joined by others in search of the fortunes to be made in salt, including W.W. Cox, William Norman, Alexander Robinson, John Gregory, William Imlay, Darwin Peckham, and Milton Langdon. With the passage of the Homestead Act in 1862, a large number of settlers began to arrive.

Salt was a scarce commodity, about equal to flour in price. Not only was salt a dietary necessity and seasoning, but also it was virtually the only available method of preserving meat. Emigrants went out of their way to stop, and settlers came from hundreds of miles to replenish their meager supplies.

The salt, though often simply scraped from the ground as crystals, was found naturally in the form of brine. Underground springs dissolved rock-salt deposits which subsequently came to the surface as salt water. Today the primary basin of the 1850s is under Capital Beach Lake, but at that time the area was dry and the land visibly parched and barren. Augustus F. Harvey reported in a pamphlet published in 1869 that you could stick your arm into the cracks in the ground, up to the elbow. Then a mysterious thing occurred: twice a day, like clockwork, the basin flooded with brine to a depth of two to three inches. When the "tide" receded, the brine would disappear into the cracks, leaving a white crystalline film behind from solar evaporation. Over the course of days or weeks,

this would accumulate to a depth of three to four inches and could be simply scraped up and used without further refinement. The problem came when it rained, dissolving the salt and sending it back below. It was not uncommon for men to travel several days in hopes of harvesting salt only to see it dissolve and wash away before their eyes.

The best and surest commercial method of producing salt was to build a fire and boil the brine in a large kettle. The problem was the paucity of wood for fuel in the immediate area. Irving, on approaching the basin in 1835, noted that "there was a degree of pain, of loneliness, in the scene. A tree would have been a companion, a friend. It would have taken away the very desolation which hung round us, and would have thrown an air of sociability over the face of nature; but there were none." More than anything else, it was the dearth of trees that made the salt ventures commercial failures. In order to work with the sun, a system of reservoirs was constructed of timbers. From there the brine was pumped into large wooden vats with covers to protect the crop from dilution by rain. About a half ton of salt could be salvaged per vat in a week's time, but the process was still too slow to be commercially successful. Before the lake was reflooded in the mid-1960s, a group of Boy Scouts investigated the flats and found several of the timbered ponds still intact. These are undoubtedly still there under several feet of water awaiting future archeological expeditions.

As mentioned earlier, probably the first commercial salt manufacturer to settle in the area was Captain W.T. Donovan, a representative of the Crescent Salt Company of Plattsmouth. His 1856 claim at the mouth of Salt Creek did not prove out, however, and he soon removed to Yankee Hill. By 1861 several firms were in business. One producer was historian Samuel Cox, who noted that people were coming from as far as Des Moines and trading everything from flour and eggs to cast-iron stoves for salt. In 1862 John Gregory, who was to become the first postmaster in the area, arrived to try his hand and is said to have maximized production at nearly two tons a day.

As early as 1796 it was the practice of the federal government to protect such salt lands from sale or private production. A specific act of Congress in 1864 set the Lancaster basin aside as state land patents. Unfortunately, the related survey was not recorded in the plat of the area, and the obvious questions remained as to whether the lands were reserved from sale or were for sale at the discretion of the state. Governor Butler gave a state lease, subject to legislative approval, to A.C. Tichenor. After some disputes Mr. Tichenor sold his interest to Horace Smith of the weapons manufacturing firm of Smith and Wesson. Smith then turned production over to his nephew James Hebbard of Nebraska City. Before these claims J. Sterling Morton had secured federal land patents but held them only from 1859 to 1862, when the Secretary of the Interior canceled them after realizing that the state had been assigned title. When Morton learned, some 10 years later, of the Tichenor and Smith leases, he realized that he might still have some claim to what was suddenly a profitable-looking piece of property. The case had become so complicated that by 1870 it appeared that only a court could determine the true ownership.

Morton figured that possession was indeed nine points of the law and on December 24 convinced Ed Roggen, later secretary of state of Nebraska, to accompany him as he set off for the flats. As the weather had been cloudy for several weeks, the salt business was shut down, with the works left unattended and unlocked. Morton and Roggen had no trouble at all in entering one of the buildings to await legal action which would discover them in possession. The owners of the cabin heard of the trespass almost at once and on advice of counsel watched and waited. The night being cold, Morton and Roggen soon slipped out and brought in some logs to start a fire. This was just what the owners were waiting for. Armed with a warrant and the town marshal, they swooped down

Above: The first cabins in Lancaster County were usually dugouts covered with poles and sod, or sod houses whose 18-inch-thick walls provided good insulation against the fierce winters and summer heat in the prairie.

Right: John Gillespie was the first state auditor and a member of the Capital Commission (with Governor David Butler and Secretary of State Thomas P. Kennard).

and arrested the pair, not for trespassing but for stealing their firewood, which was worth $10 a cord! As the next day was Christmas Sunday, the justice of the peace released the pair on their own recognizance till Monday, at which time the charges were dropped. Within two weeks Morton sued the marshal for $20,000 for malicious prosecution and false imprisonment and was awarded $100.

Morton pursued his claim to the land through a series of complicated court cases until the U.S. Supreme Court ultimately ruled against him. The entire proceeding then became moot when Morton purchased land at Hutchinson, Kansas, where caves furnished easily mined salt of excellent quality for the Morton Salt Company. As late as 1886 others continued to attempt to make a living at salt refining in Lancaster County but what had long been hoped would be a sound basis for local industry was finally abandoned and the basin was flooded in 1895 by damming Oak Creek to provide a recreational lake.

Popular legend has it that on July 4, 1863, one of the early salt settlers, W.W. Cox, was out gathering gooseberries when he came upon a party headed by Elder J.M. Young of the Methodist Church, along with Luke Lavender, Peter Schamp, the Reverend Dr. J.M. McKesson, E.W. Warnes, and Jacob Dawson. The band had come up from Nebraska City in search of a site for a Methodist Protestant female seminary.

On July 10 Elder Young returned and settled east of the salt basins. The land he bought consisted of a quarter section (160 acres) running from present-day 5th to 12th Street and from O to Vine Street. He paid $140 in cash from the seminary association's $500 treasury for this parcel and later added another 80-acre tract. He immediately platted the town site of Lancaster and set up a street system, numbering the north-south streets from 1st to 12th. Beginning with the old cattle trail, he named the southern boundary Locust (now O Street), and the east-west streets proceeded northward as High, College, Lincoln, Main, Washington, Saline,

Elder J.M. Young, pictured seated at left with his family, arrived in Lancaster County in 1863 seeking a site for a Methodist colony and female seminary. The land on which he built his home contained the area that the state surveyor felt would make an ideal site for the first state capitol. Although many other area landowners donated land to the state to encourage its bringing the capital to Lancaster County, Lavender held out for $1,000 cash, along with replacement of the four-square-block tract.

Nebraska, and North. The entire city was 12 blocks by eight blocks. He then deeded about half the city, in alternate-lot parcels, to the seminary association. A good portion of the remainder was set aside as school and county land.

Standing at about 5th and Locust (now 9th and O), an observer in 1863 could survey a vast area, as the grade was then 15 feet higher and there were no trees or buildings in any direction. Several creek beds, usually dry, crossed the plat, and wild animals, including deer, antelope, coyotes, and even buffalo, could be spotted. The salt flats to the northwest shone white in the reflected sun. A plum thicket grew about where the seminary would be built. A lone elm west of the present Burlington depot and a few honey locusts on Oak and

Salt creeks were the only trees. The horizon in all directions appeared as the rim of a saucer, with the village site at the bottom.

Late in 1864 John Gillespie, Nebraska's first state auditor, traveling by steamboat to Nebraska City, made friends with a son of Elder Young, on furlough from the army. Mr. Young met his son at the dock and was reintroduced to Gillespie, whom he had known when both men had lived in Nebraska City. Gillespie was amazed to learn that Young no longer lived there and asked why on earth he had chosen to relocate in the wilderness. Elder Young replied, "Oh, I am founding a colony out there and am building a female seminary. We will soon have the county seat, and will have the capital there some day."

Gillespie knew that Young was an optimist, but he must have thought his friend a bit daft in opening a ladies' school in a city with only one female and, further, to believe that the capital would ever locate in an area that was plumb on the edge of the Great American Desert, so desolate that virtually no settlement existed.

Some time in 1864 Young began constructing the first building of any consequence, at 6th and High. The seminary was a two-story structure of native red sandstone, about 30 by 50 feet. In August the seminary, though uncompleted, hosted a debate between congressional candidates J. Sterling Morton and T.M. Marquett with an audience of about 50. The first term of public school was held in the unfinished seminary in the fall of that year by H.W. Merrill, who had about eight students. It had been reported that Mr. Merrill also taught four young ladies in seminary classes, but this appears apocryphal. The following term Mrs. Merrill took over the duties in the dirt-floored room, with the provision that her family be allowed to live in the building and that she be allowed to bring her baby to classes. This experiment was to be short-lived, however, as the interior of the building burned in 1867, and although school was offered in a church building in the same block, it proved unsuccessful.

There was never even a glimmer of reestablishing the seminary after its ill-fated inception. The Methodist Protestant Church, its sponsor, was collapsing. The Methodist Protestant brick church at 12th and K, the first masonry church in the city, was completed, but a service was never held there. Apparently everyone quickly saw the folly of the idea, and most of the Methodist Protestant colony left.

Meanwhile Jacob Dawson built a double-walled, dirt-floored log cabin on the south side of Locust at 3rd (now 7th and O) and was appointed postmaster on September 15, 1864. His federal salary was fixed at seven dollars a year. The delivery arrived at Yankee Hill once a month by government wagon via the Oregon Trail Cutoff. Dawson felt that because he had to

Luke Lavender—shown above, with his wife shown above left— arrived in 1863 with Elder Young's party, was one of Lincoln's first settlers, and built one of the city's first homes.

ride that distance to pick up the mail, the salary was insufficient. His complaint was answered by a raise in pay to $12 annually. The question of whether Dawson's cabin was the first to be completed is answered by the fact that the territorial court was held there in the fall of 1864. The court noted that Dawson's home was the only completed building, meaning that Luke Lavender's cabin at 12th and Locust (14th and O) must have been second, not first as the plaque on the site suggests.

A major blizzard began as court was announced, and Dawson had to borrow virtually all the coffee and food in the village to "keep the court." Lincoln historian A.B. Hayes recounts in his 1889 *History of the City of Lincoln, Nebraska* that Judge Elmer S. Dundy heard Mr. Pottenger of Plattsmouth argue for the territory that a Mr. Pemberton "had shot his revolver into Mr. Bird's house {chicken coop}, and thumped Bird {the rooster} with it afterward, owing to some difficulty Pemberton had had with one of Bird's daughters {a pullet}. The Birds had talked, and Pemberton 'did up' the father in consequence." A grand jury was impaneled and charged Pemberton with malicious assault with intent to kill. Unfortunately, nearly all eligible jurors in the area were already serving the court on the grand jury. Because there was no jail and not enough additional men to constitute a jury, the case was dismissed.

By 1867 the rest of the community consisted of Elder Young's house between 3rd and 4th on Locust (7th and O), which had a sod roof and board floor while most cabins in the Great Plains had shingled roofs and dirt floors; the Reverend Dr. John M. McKesson's dugout just north of 9th and North (about 12th and Vine); S.B. Galey's small stone building at 7th and High (10th and P); and Jacob Dawson's new house at 6th and Locust (virtually the middle of the block bounded by N, O, 9th, and 10th streets). As 1867 began, few in the Nebraska Territory save the most visionary could predict what vast changes would be thrust upon the tiny village of Lancaster and its 30 residents within a few months.

CHAPTER III

A NEW STATE CAPITAL

On April 4, 1867, Governor David Butler issued a call for a meeting of the Nebraska State Legislature. In the records the resulting session, which convened May 16, is termed the "third session" because of the inclusion of two meetings held on July 4, 1866, and February 20, 1867. For most purposes, however, this session, which was held in the old territorial capitol at Omaha, was the first session under statehood. Governor Butler listed 45 areas that he felt needed legislative attention. Although capital removal was officially item number 19, there is little doubt that all concerned knew it to be one of the most controversial and important on the list. The South Platters had been politically upstaged time and again, but now they had a majority in both houses and had elected one of their own as governor. Their day was at hand.

Through the efforts of Senator Augustus Harvey, Senator William Presson of Richardson County introduced Senate Bill No. 44, titled "An Act to Provide for the Seat of Government of the State of Nebraska and for the Erection of Public Buildings Thereat." The bill called for a commission—to be made up of Governor David Butler, Secretary of State Thomas P. Kennard, and State Auditor John Gillespie—to examine specified lands to consist of at least 640 acres (one square mile) and to select such lands on or before July 15 (later amended to September 15) as a capital site. The legislative committee, though anxious to have the removal dealt with quickly, felt that it would be wise to

move the seat as far west as practical so as not to have the question arise on future occasions. As the western boundary of Lancaster County was thought of as the terminus of the Great American Desert, it seemed an easy conclusion that little if any population would ever exist west of that line. The legislature therefore stipulated that their choices were to be limited to those lands belonging to the state within Seward, Lancaster, Butler, and Saunders counties. After the site selection, the land was to be surveyed and platted, with lots in alternate blocks being auctioned to provide a fund for the erection of a capitol, not to cost more than $50,000 and to be completed by November 1, 1868, as well as a state university, a state penitentiary, and later a state insane hospital. The site for the seat of the state government was then to be named Capital City.

Although the South Platters had a clear, though small, majority, the outcome was not beyond dispute, as party lines were being ignored on this occasion. Senator J.N.H. Patrick of Douglas County had an idea. Senator Mills Reeves of Otoe County was one of the prime instigators of the removalists, and although Nebraska City was known as a stopping point on John Brown's Underground Railway, Reeves had been a slaveholder and champion of the South until the recent end of the Civil War. Patrick felt that if he could rattle the bill's promoters he might yet win the capital for Omaha. Chief among Reeves' dislikes was Abraham Lincoln, whom he

The first state capitol in Lincoln is pictured about 1870 with a horse-drawn coach in the foreground. From the author's collection

31

THE FOUNDING OF
LINCOLN
ON JULY 29 1867
IN SESSION AT
THE FRONTIER HOME OF
CAPT. W. T. DONOVAN
LOCATED 166 FEET NORTH
638 FEET EAST OF THIS SPOT

THE NEBRASKA STATE
CAPITAL COMMISSION
DAVID BUTLER, GOVERNOR
JOHN J. GILLESPIE, AUDITOR
THOMAS P. KENNARD
SECY. OF STATE
LOCATED LINCOLN
CAPITAL CITY OF NEBRASKA
ON THIS PRAIRIE

ERECTED BY NEBRASKA SOCIETY
SONS OF THE AMERICAN REVOLUTION
JULY 29 1927

had repeatedly and loudly denounced. The plan was simplicity itself: Patrick moved to amend the bill, substituting the word "Lincoln" for "Capital City," certain that Reeves would vote against the bill merely to keep the name of Lincoln from being forever linked with Nebraska. Reeves, whom Patrick had just referred to as a Copperhead in order to ensure that his blood would be adequately circulating, jumped to his feet. Some reports indicate that Reeves actually jumped up on his desk. This is not hard to believe, since the last territorial session had been punctuated with shotguns, revolvers, and mop handles. At any rate, he shouted, "Mr. President," and having been given the floor continued, to everyone's surprise, "I second the motion of the senator from Douglas." The bill thus passed the senate easily on June 10, eight to five with Senator Patrick on the negative. Thus the city of Lincoln was named, not as an honor to the great martyred President and leader of the Union cause, but rather because of a poorly laid political scheme that backfired.

There was some editorial grumbling, particularly on the part of Omaha, that the new capital would be as far from the center of population as the old, merely in a new location. A question as to the proper bonding of the commission was raised but never really pressed, and on Thursday, June 18, the three commissioners, along with Augustus Harvey and several members of the press, assembled at Nebraska City preparatory to examine the lands suggested as capital sites. Leaving after lunch the following day, the troop arrived at Syracuse in time for supper and decided to spend the night there. On the 20th they arrived at Saline City, also known as Yankee Hill, and there stayed with John Cadman. The loss of the county seat had left Mr. Cadman more than a bit disappointed, and he intended to secure the capital at any cost. It is a safe assumption that after spending four days and nights with the Cadmans at Silver Lake Farm (now about 400 West Calvert Street), the commission was most favorably impressed with the city. It was not only the largest settlement they were to visit, having a population of about 100, but also it had a commanding situation above the Salt Creek flood plain, was on the Oregon Trail Cutoff/Lushbaugh Stage north-south route, and was close to wood and the salt flats.

On the 22nd the Capital Commission moved down Salt Creek to visit the village of Lancaster. Here they were greeted by Captain Donovan, local representative of the Cresent Salt Company. His cabin, about a block west and a bit north of the seminary, was particularly large for the area and even had a second story. It was here that the commission decided to perform their final deliberations. There was little to examine in the area save the salt flats, which were a potential industrial base for the capital. What did interest the commission was the willingness of the Methodist Protestant Church to turn over all their land holdings in the community to the state, should Lancaster receive the official choice. The 23rd saw the commission head east from the village of Lancaster to the Stevens Creek area, where they spent the night.

On the 24th the party surveyed the area around Ashland and found what they thought might make an acceptable location. This tract later became the site of the Saunders County courthouse until it was moved to the city of Wahoo some years later. That night they stayed in an unfinished two-story brick building in what was to become the business district. Governor Butler, being the senior member of the gathering, stayed downstairs, while the rest of the commission and the reporters spent the night on the second story. The governor was definitely favored by the arrangement, as the ground floor was nearly completed, including screens on the windows, while the upper rooms had no such niceties. In summer along the river bottoms when the sun went down, then as now, the mosquitoes came out. The members of the press reported a couple of days later, when they filed their first story for the newspapers, that although the governor spent a quiet night, those on the second floor were nearly eaten alive and

spent a vigorous night of exercise. Five days later there would be one vote for Ashland and two opposed on the first location ballot.

As they moved west to complete their tour, the commission spent the night of the 25th in Butler County at the home of J.D. Brown. On the 26th they visited the headwaters of Oak Creek and Seward, camping near Milford, and on the 27th returned to Saline City. Visiting with each of the party, John Cadman learned that the popular choice was still the Yankee Hill/Saline City vicinity. Mr. Cadman should have left well enough alone, but he feared that because Nebraska City was so greatly in favor of Yankee Hill a compromise location might be chosen by the commission in order to placate the rest of the South Platters. In order to promote his city further, Cadman decided to "fire both barrels" and made what was to prove another political error—he asked his wife to prepare a feast for the last evening before final deliberations commenced. Mrs. Cadman, herself an excellent cook, marshaled help from her sister and a number of other women in the area. The huge meal, which featured fried chicken and ice cream, was served up on the east lawn of Cadman's Silver Lake Farm.

This plaque (opposite), mounted on the east wall of the Burlington station in 1927, commemorates the founding of Lincoln. The Capital Commission met in the attic of Captain W.T. Donovan's cabin to decide the site of Nebraska's capital city. David Butler (below left) was Nebraska's first state governor and a senior member of the Capital Commission. In 1871 he was impeached and removed from office, but Butler was later elected state senator and then nearly reelected governor.

After again spending the night as Cadman's guests, the commission was escorted back to Lancaster the following morning. The small parade of wagons which accompanied them did not even wait to hear the verdict but returned to Yankee Hill. The capital was surely theirs now.

After preliminary discussion, a ballot was taken in the conference room established in Captain Donovan's attic. Ashland received one yea and two nays. After further deliberation, a unanimous ballot was cast, and the commissioners left the cabin to make their decision public. J.C.F. McKesson, nephew of the Reverend J.M. McKesson, was a boy at the time. He later recalled, before the Nebraska Territorial Pioneers' Association in 1917, that he, along with "several other boys had been swimming and fishing in what was then the public swimming pool, called Willow Bend...in the old channel of Salt Creek, and came by...with a string of fish." About 15 townspeople were gathered to hear that not Yankee Hill but Lancaster had received the commissioners' vote to become the state capital.

The reason Ashland failed as a potential site was the mosquitoes, pure and simple. What today would be little more than a nuisance was then an insurmountable obstacle. The vote against Yankee Hill was considerably more interesting. Yankee Hill had at least one strike against it by being the singular choice of the Nebraska City faction, whereas Lancaster represented a compromise acceptable to virtually all the South Platters. One of the decisive factors against Yankee Hill, however, was a combination of John Cadman's reputation and the sumptuous dinner served to the commission the previous evening. Many might initially wonder why the menu served that evening would be worth historical mention, but the ice cream was reportedly the first ever made in Nebraska. To prepare ice cream late in the summer, before artificial refrigeration, required the use of ice sawed from ponds the previous winter and stored in sawdust or straw. To make ice cream would undoubtedly have

strained the supplies of the entire community. This sacrifice impressed the commissioners greatly. In matching the ice cream with John Cadman's political reputation, the commissioners agreed to a man that it constituted bribery and they unanimously agreed to vote against Yankee Hill on those grounds. Thus the choice of Lancaster as the state capital, it could be said, was a matter of mosquitoes and ice cream.

Although formal announcement of Lancaster as the capital and establishment of the city of Lincoln did not come until August 14, 1867, Augustus Harvey and Anselmo B. Smith immediately began the official plat of the new city of Lincoln, which was completed August 26, 1867.

It was not until this point that Omaha, which had been busily prospering as a commercial and transportation hub, began to realize that with the loss of the capital a great political advantage had likewise slipped away. The local politicians began looking for loopholes and schemes to discredit the commission and win the capital back—attacks that in some forms continue to the present. One of the provisions of the removal act stipulated that within 10 days the commissioners had to post bonds to the state supreme court, which would in turn be passed to the state treasurer. This was done, except that the bonds were not turned over to the treasurer within the 10 days. Detractors now claimed that the commission was not a legal body and had no right to choose a capital, survey it, and sell the property. If they proceeded with the scheme, the treasurer, under threat of enforcing legal action, would simply hold the money collected so that no capitol could be constructed from the funds. Alerted by published warning, the commission promised to hang onto auction proceeds and pay contractors directly, neatly bypassing the treasurer.

The plat itself was well thought out, with streets laid out in grids, numbered for north-south streets and lettered for east-west streets. The house-numbering system began at O Street and progressed in hundreds, indicating blocks, to the south and north. The east-west numbering system commenced at First Street and progressed to the east with hundreds again representing blocks. This simple device allowed for expansion and variations, making Lincoln perhaps the easiest city of its size in the United States in which to find a given address. Blocks and lots were set aside for state, county, and city buildings, schools, parks, 10 religious denominations, a market square, and three lodges.

The legislative requirement for a tract of not less than 640 acres was easily surpassed; the final plat totaled 960 acres. The major contributors of land, in addition to the previously held state land, were Julian and Julia Metcalf, Jacob and Edith Dawson, John and Alice Young, Joseph (also referred to as John) Giles, and the U.S. government. Approximately 320 acres came from the trustees of the Lancaster Seminary. One hundred and sixty acres of the seminary's land, exclusive of a few lots that had been conveyed to private owners, were termed the "old townsite of Lancaster." Because the old plat of Lancaster was never vacated and the new plat of Lincoln was simply overlaid, any lots in the present city of Lincoln lying between 7th and 14th streets and between O Street and the U Street alley must be abstracted back to determine how they were represented in Lancaster.

The next step, as stipulated by the legislature, was to advertise the lots for sale and conduct the auction. The advertisements were issued on August 17, with the sale scheduled to begin on September 17 in Lincoln. Although an excellent auctioneer and a brass band had been hired, the weather was totally uncooperative, and the sale actually commenced on September 18. It was only with considerable difficulty that one single lot finally was hammered down to J.G. Miller for Block 23 at a 25-cent advance over the state's $40 minimum. It was later reported that early lots went for 25 and 50 cents, but actually each tract had a minimum value established by the state and the figures reported were the amount bid over

This advertisement, published in 1872, called for a lottery to finance a city hospital. The proposed lottery was apparently never held, and Lincoln General Hospital did not open until 1925.

those minimums.

Things looked glum that evening when a "council of war" was convened at the Donovan house by the capital commissioners and a Nebraska City syndicate headed by James Sweet. The capital commissioners had originally agreed not to bid at the sale for fear it might later appear they were profiteering and attempting to push other investors to bid on the strength of the commissioners' confidence. Now they agreed that if they did not enter the bidding, it would appear as though even those who chose the capital did not have enough confidence in the plan to buy lots for themselves. Mr. Sweet committed his syndicate to $10,000, which they would use to open every lot at its minimum value until the pool was exhausted. The commissioners also agreed to join the sale personally to display their confidence. The group further agreed, without any legal standing, that if at least $25,000 in sales were not forthcoming, their original $10,000 in bids would be returned. The first five days' sales were reported variously at about $34,000 and more than $44,000; at any rate the scheme was a grand success. The original plan was to hold sales in Lincoln, Nebraska City, Omaha, Plattsmouth, Brownville, and again in Lincoln if necessary to complete the process. By the time the Omaha leg of the sale was completed, it was deemed unnecessary to go to Plattsmouth or Brownville. The lots designated for sale were appraised at $68,000 with the first schedule yielding $63,475, or $13,146 over the minimums established. The expenses for the sale, including $1,186.65 for the commissioners, $1,135.05 for advertising, $720 for auctioneers, and $1,803.25 for the survey, totaled $5,296.65. True to their word, the commissioners did not pass on the funds collected from the sale; when pressed, particularly for the advertising accounts, the commission simply forwarded sufficient money to pay the outstanding bills and directly pocketed their own expenses.

On August 28, 1867, the commission placed ads in Omaha, Plattsmouth, and Nebraska City newspapers calling for

architects to present plans for a suitable building to accommodate the six legislative offices and two houses of the legislature, the cost of which should not exceed $40,000. No replies were forthcoming, and the advertisement was placed in the Chicago *Tribune*. From this placement one lone entry appeared from Chicago architect James Morris. Subsequently Taggart and Craig, an architectural firm in Nebraska City, also submitted a plan, but no further mention of their design appears. On the 10th of October the commission officially accepted the plans of Mr. Morris. The total size of the building was to be 160 feet by 70 feet, with walls 50 feet high and a tower of 80 feet, surmounted by a 40-foot cupola. The central tower would be 25 feet square. On the first floor were to be a 20-by-22-foot vestibule, a library, five executive rooms, and several smaller offices. The second floor would house both legislative chambers, the Supreme Court, the governor's office, four committee rooms, and several smaller offices. Over the central area would be an additional floor giving access to the observers' galleries around the representative and senate halls and four additional committee rooms. The facing was specified as native limestone; this would result in a higher cost than planned but would offer a much more pleasing building. As the state and its offices grew, provision was made for additions to the north and south with tower corners. Mr. Morris was also appointed to supervise construction, and he advertised for construction bids. Again only one real application was received, and on January 11, 1868, the bid of $49,000 from Joseph Ward of Chicago was accepted.

Well before Mr. Ward was accepted as contractor, Mr. Morris had ground broken on November 10, 1867, under the direction of F. Morton Donovan, the first child born in Lancaster. With this done, laborers began digging trenches for the footings, while Mr. Ward began gathering his own stonemasons and other skilled laborers, which were unavailable in Lincoln. The stonemasons arrived three days ahead of Mr. Ward, expecting to find stone already

Dr. N.C. Gilbert, who came to Lincoln from Nebraska City, operated this hardware, book, paint, and drug store in addition to maintaining his medical practice on the northwest corner of 9th and O streets. The gentleman in the middle of the street was Lincoln's first artist.

cut and ready to be worked. The only visible evidence of any construction was the trenches. By the time Mr. Ward showed up, his workers were ready to lynch him, fearing they might wait weeks or months without stone and hence without pay. Mr. Ward assured them that their wages of $4.50 a day would be paid whether they worked or not. While Mr. Ward began scouting out suitable stone, the masons proceeded to build a sod dormitory on the capitol grounds. Most of the stone examined was worthless for building purposes, but finally a farmer's quarry 17 miles north of Beatrice yielded a quantity of magnesia limestone which was substituted for the blue limestone on Salt Creek when it proved "shelly." The new problem was moving the stone nearly 50 miles. On July 30, 1869, Mr. Morris appealed to the commission to allow nearly $20,000 in excess costs for construction, primarily because of the unforeseen

problems encountered with native materials. Labor and financing problems also plagued the construction, but after the election of 1868 Governor Butler announced that the 1869 legislative session would be held in the new capitol.

By mid-December 1868, Mr. Gillespie was satisfied with the capitol construction and quietly began laying plans to move the library and other physical properties from the old territorial building to Lincoln. He hired J.T. Beach of Lincoln, who subcontracted with a Mr. Carr and Luke Cropsey to provide the necessary wagons, horses, and manpower. The agreed price was $100; a $40 check on the state treasury was paid in advance, with the balance to be collected when the move was completed. Mr. Beach, driving a two-horse team, and Mr. Carr with a four-horse team, set out Friday morning. Late in the afternoon they arrived at Ashland and, after serious problems with ice floes, finally crossed the

Platte River at Forest Crossing and there spent the night. At 11 o'clock Saturday morning they arrived in Omaha. They left the wagons at the "Old Checkered Barn," checked into the Douglas House, and sought out Auditor Gillespie at the capitol. The plan was to load the property on Sunday and leave before daybreak Monday so that any Omahans who might think unkindly about the move would not even know about it until after the fact. All went well until Saturday night, when the cash brought by Beach, Carr, and Cropsey was expended. They then attempted to persuade a local saloon keeper to cash the $40 warrant. The check, drawn by the state on a Lincoln account, was viewed with great suspicion; the merchant tentatively offered to cash it for a 10-percent fee, considerably angering Mr. Beach. Fortunately, Mr. Gillespie was called on to cash the check, or the secrecy of the mission might well have been breached.

At 4 o'clock Monday morning the two wagons left Omaha under cover of dark and the beginnings of a snowstorm. As they turned onto Farnam Street, they were stopped by U.S. Marshal Yost, and it was feared they were to be thwarted before even reaching the city limits. Mr. Yost, however, quietly loaded a cider barrel labeled "T.P. Kennard" on one wagon without comment, and they were off again. Knowing of the difficulty of recrossing the river at Ashland, particularly with the now heavy snow, they decided to cross at La Platte, just above Plattsmouth, where there was a ferry operated by the Kimball brothers. This short trip occupied most of the day.

Unknown to the moving party, the Kimball brothers were not only profiteers but in sympathy with the Omaha faction. Before they were able to effect the crossing, one of the brothers sabotaged the pulley system while the other headed for Omaha to warn of the "theft of the library." On the following morning the Lincoln party was joined by Tom Keller, an outlaw later shot down at Elkhorn. Unsavory a character as he may have been, Mr. Keller's political leanings were with the Lincoln removalists. He managed to repair the pulley system, and though they had to abandon the ferry 100 feet shy of the south shore, they did manage to cross the river by 10 o'clock.

As the snowstorm grew in intensity, they were able to go only as far as Stove Creek, near Greenwood, before dark. Here they approached a one-room log cabin and asked for shelter. As they had no cash and their story may have seemed a bit unlikely to the settler and his wife, they were refused. After unsuccessfully attempting to camp in the farmer's haystack, the three finally convinced the man that they would send payment back from Lincoln. Finally on Wednesday the state seal, library, desks, chairs, and miscellaneous property were unloaded at their new home.

Because of the snow and the lack of publicity, it was several days before John R. Meredith visited Gillespie at the now empty territorial office in Omaha and discovered the capitol property gone. Meredith stormed out and returned with General S.A. Strickland from Fort Omaha, who demanded that the library be returned. General Strickland wired the Secretary of the Interior of the United States, who was responsible for territorial but not state questions, and was subsequently informed that the movement was indeed in order. In an interview in 1888 Mr. Carr claimed that the state never did pay the movers the $60 promised after they were finished. If this is true, and if Mr. Beach did send payment back to the homesteader for their night's lodgings at Greenwood, the state got quite a bargain and, with interest, probably owes a considerable sum to the heirs of the three men.

With the completion of the statehouse, the legislature turned to the establishment of a university, an insane hospital, and later a penitentiary. The state senate provided for the charter of the University of Nebraska and a building to house it in February 1869. In April plans were advertised for, and on June 5 lot sales began again, raising nearly $30,000 the first day, assuring the commission that funding would be no problem, as the legislature had authorized $100,000. Within 11 days the *Nebraska Commonwealth* noted that Mr. R.D. Silver of the firm of Silver and Sons of Logansport, Indiana, had arrived and begun construction of a brickyard that would produce 12,000 bricks a day on the 12-acre university site. The plans of J.M. McBird, also of Logansport, Indiana, for a Franco-Italian building were accepted on June 2, but not until August 18, 1869, was the construction contract awarded to Silver and Sons, for $128,480. Two discrepancies are at once apparent: Mr. Silver was preparing to manufacture brick on the site nearly two months before he officially won the contract, and the resulting contract was for $28,480 more than authorized by the legislature. The Nebraska press was at once polarized, one side challenging the contract and the other defending the extra expense as necessary to ensure having a first-rate building. Amidst the questions, the cornerstone was laid on September 23,

1869, with a brass band from Omaha, a banquet provided by the citizens of Lincoln, and speeches by the Masons who were in charge of the ceremony, as well as several additional officials of dubious oratorical skill. The festivities ended with a street dance that lasted from 10 o'clock until four the following morning.

On January 6, 1871, the regents toured the nearly completed building and gave it their seal of approval. On learning that some of the foundation stone was identical with the material that was already proving to be of poor quality at the statehouse, however, they asked a committee of three architects to reexamine the construction. The report, made public on June 23, pronounced the building "safe for the present and probably for years to come" but did suggest that some repairs be made even before the building was to see its first students. These repairs were effected, and the first classes were held on September 6. In March 1873 further concerns were voiced as to the stability of the building, and another architectural survey called for a new foundation for the chapel. In 1877 the chancellor was pressured into yet another investigation, which concluded that the walls could come down around the ears of the students at any time. This time the recommendation was to tear the building down and erect a new one at a cost of about $60,000, with the city of Lincoln putting up $40,000 of the amount. Nebraska City immediately offered to provide a building for the university, and Omaha joined in supporting the move. The citizens of Lincoln, seeing the advantage slipping from their grasp, quickly hired engineers from Chicago and Dubuque to examine the structure. Their findings suggested that the problems could easily be repaired. After consultation with the regents, the citizens of Lincoln paid for the various repairs, which amounted to $6,012.

The first university had but one college, that of Literature, Science, and Arts. Eight students were enrolled for the first term, along with 12 "irregulars" and 110 in the Latin, or preparatory, school. No tuition was charged at the land-grant university,

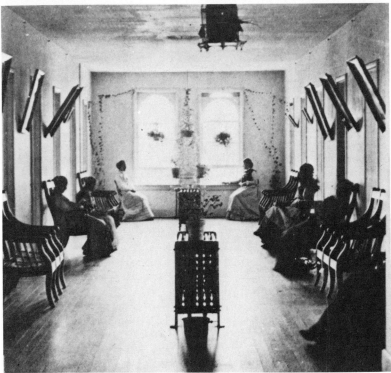

but the charter allowed for a matriculation fee of five dollars to be paid into the library fund when a student was admitted. Although some rooms were at first provided on the upper floors, the university decided against the dormitory system, as room and board were easily found in the community for less than five dollars a week. Books were provided by the school at cost. There is some evidence that the state legislature was less than impressed with the institution, referring to the university as "Lincoln High School." The first commencement was held on June 26, 1872, when an honorary LL.D. was conferred on Bishop R.H. Clarkson of the Episcopal Church; but the first regular graduate, J. Stuart Dales of East Rochester, Ohio, did not receive his degree until 1873. Dales followed the family of the university's first chancellor, Allen R. Benton. Dales was soon engaged to Grace Benton, the chancellor's daughter, and in 1875 joined the administration of the university. The following year Dales was made secretary to the board of regents and served the university's business office for more than 50 years.

The state penitentiary's first buildings at 14th Street and Pioneers Boulevard, pictured here at the turn of the century, were built on land donated by Captain W.T. Donovan. Donovan wanted to be sure that the institution was as far as possible from the main settlement of Lincoln.

At about the same time as provision was being made for the university, the legislature also provided for the "State Lunatic Asylum" at Lincoln. While a few patients were housed at the state hospital in Iowa, additional lots in Lincoln were put up for sale to provide the $50,000 appropriation for Nebraska's own hospital. A site of 160 acres just north of the village of Yankee Hill, southwest of Lincoln, was chosen, and work on the foundation was begun even before a contract was let, "to save time." The plans of Professor D. Winchell of Chicago were approved, and as Mr. Ward was virtually finished with the capitol, he was awarded the construction contract. The job was to be completed by

December 1, 1870, at a cost of $137,000. The facility was occupied on December 22 after damage from a small fire was repaired. The legislature, again concerned about the quality of construction, appointed a committee to examine the building in March 1871. The investigators found that the foundation was in poor and rapidly deteriorating condition, but their report was to carry little weight as the hospital burned to the ground on April 17. Mr. Silver, having completed the university, was hired to rebuild the hospital for $72,000 from the proceeds of the $96,000 insurance policy.

The third institution built by the state in its new capital was the penitentiary. Land for the institution had been proferred by W.T. Donovan and G.H. Hilton in 1867 as an inducement to locate the capital. The site was one of little value, lying in a flood plain, and was thought to be far enough south of the city to be completely isolated in case of a prison

By 1935 there were more than 1,000 patients at the state hospital and several additional buildings, including the one pictured. Patients also began maintaining their own vegetable gardens and stock operations to help offset the cost of their residency.

Above: This photo, taken in 1876 from the roof of the Centennial Opera House looking to the southwest, pictures the U.S. Land Office in the center of the view and Bohanan's Livery directly across the street.

Right: When this group portrait of Lincoln residents was made in 1874, the city claimed a population of nearly 8,000.

Opposite: The north side of P Street is shown in 1873, looking west from 10th. On the right is the first home of the First National Bank. At the far end of the block is the Methodist Seminary building, here rebuilt as the Cadman House Hotel.

uprising or breakout. In June 1870, with all of the state's other projects proceeding well, attention was turned to construction of the state prison. By July a small brown sandstone building was hastily readied to house 37 convicts. This temporary structure stood for many years within the completed compound, serving as a shop, stable, and storage shed. Three prison inspectors were elected and charged with the sale of 32,044 acres of state land to finance the project. Bids were let, and W.H.B. Stout and J.M. Jamison were awarded the $312,000 contract. Prison labor was then put into service quarrying and cutting magnesia limestone from the Saltillo quarries 12 miles south of the city. On April 17, 1871, the day the asylum burned, 10 of the prisoners effected a break by drilling through the wooden door of the temporary facility and turning the key that had been left in the outside of the lock. The penitentiary was completed in 1876 and, unlike the other early state projects, remained in constant use until it was razed in 1982, at which time portions of the original wall and guard tower were among the oldest structures in the county.

In his 1930 pamphlet, *Prairie Capital,* historian E.P. Brown observed, with tongue in cheek, that the capital city was obviously an appropriate site for all the various state institutions:

The solons had justified their claims to wisdom in erecting in one legislative day both University and Asylum. The Asylum would be needed to provide teachers for the University. The University would be needed to provide inmates for the Asylum. Opponents of the whole set-up admitted that a University was needed to instruct the fools who wanted the Asylum; and that the Asylum was needed for the nitwits who thought the state needed or could ever have a University. Both sides agreed upon the necessity for a prison. It would be needed to confine the criminal other side.

One might also add that any individual not fitting into any of these categories would be appointed to the state legislature.

CHAPTER **IV**

THE VILLAGE BECOMES A CITY

A.E. Hargreaves came to Lincoln from England in the 1870s and was an immediate success in the grocery business. After operating a retail store on O Street and a small wholesale business on P Street, he built the large building on the southwest corner of 8th and O, which is now occupied by Schwarz Paper Company. The building is pictured circa 1885, probably on the Fourth of July.

The village of Lancaster and the first years of Lincoln's growth were built with the help of wagons, horses, and oxen. The settlers arrived in covered wagons pulled primarily by oxen; the lumber was hauled by team from Nebraska City and Garland; mail hauling and personal travel were accomplished by horse or stagecoach. The citizens were well aware, even before the new capital was established, that prosperity and progress hinged on the coming of the railroad. Towns that were bypassed more often than not withered, moved, or simply died. The *Nebraska Commonwealth* of November 23, 1867, reported that, at the urging of Elder Young, Lancaster County commissioners had authorized $100,000 in bonds, the principal to be paid to the first railroad to reach Lincoln. The state joined in two years later by offering a two-year premium of 2,000 acres of land for each mile of track completed in the state. The $100,000 offer was vetoed by the county voters, but the city authorized a $50,000 premium if the railroad should reach Lincoln before December 1, 1869. The county voters then finally approved the original $100,000 offer with the proviso that the Lincoln terminal be reached by May 13, 1870.

In June 1869 Governor Butler, the capital commission, and a representative of the Burlington and Missouri River Railroad met near Salt Creek to break ground for the railroad's imminent arrival. After it became obvious that the May 13 deadline was unrealistic, it was hoped that the arrival could be timed for the Fourth of

July 1870. On that date the steam engine *Wauhoo* managed to reach a point southwest of the present site of Havelock. Finally, on July 26, the age of steam arrived. Convinced that Lincoln's growth was now assured, Charles H. Gere, editor of the Lincoln *State Journal,* announced that the weekly publication would henceforth be a daily. The Burlington was quickly followed by the Atchison and Nebraska from Atchison, Kansas, the Midland Pacific from Nebraska City, and the Omaha and Southwestern from Omaha.

With the recent move of the U.S. Land Office from Nebraska City to Lincoln, the capital city also became a staging point for emigrants. In the spring it was common for 30 to 40 emigrant wagons to camp at Haymarket Square, but by fall the numbers quickly diminished. The Burlington, eager to dispose of its bounty from the state, established an embarkation point in Lincoln and advertised land at low prices, with low interest, minimal down payments, and free or reduced fares to emigrants who bought land. At the Emigrant House north of the present depot, land buyers, who often arrived in a boxcar containing all their possessions, family, and livestock, were offered the services of a hotel, restaurant, and laundry facility while they prepared to move to their newly acquired land.

Although Lincoln was officially incorporated in 1868, the city was not ready to commence business and failed to act on the incorporation. The process was repeated in 1869, and this time a full complement of election officials, trustees,

Above: By the time this photo was taken in 1880, the city had acquired the block of land bounded by 9th, 10th, R, and S streets for use as a public square. The old Haymarket Square at 9th and O was sold to the federal government for construction of a post office/courthouse.

Top: This A.R. Waud drawing of workers laying railroad tracks across the Great Plains appeared in the late 1850s. Lincoln became a railroad town in 1870 with the arrival of the Burlington and Missouri River Railroad.

clerks, and treasurers were duly sworn in. The city prospered: lot sales boomed, buildings sprang up, and the population grew at a geometric rate. In 1867 the village of Lancaster had a population of about 30 and contained only five or six buildings; three years later the city of Lincoln had about 2,500 people and nearly 350 buildings. John H. Ames, an early local historian, reported in the Lincoln Statesman in 1870 that the value of real property in the city was assessed at $456,956 and that nine churches, one bank, and two hotels were in operation. The capital commissioners were acknowledged leaders in the community; each built a home to show his confidence in the prairie capital. Governor Butler's mansion was on South 7th Street between Washington and Garfield, Mr. Kennard's home was at 1627 H, and Mr. Gillespie's house was directly south of Kennard's on G Street. In 1871 growth was proceeding at a rate that allowed Lincoln to organize as a city of the second class and elect its first mayor, W.F. Chapin. Unfortunately, storm clouds were already building on the horizon.

During the summer of 1870 several newspapers, particularly the Omaha Herald and the Omaha Bee, began questioning the ethics and legality of several actions of the capital commissioners. Specifically, they charged that the three had bought lots at the state sale against the orders of the legislature; that the state, under direction of the governor, had made loans to individuals from state school funds; that contracts for state buildings had been allowed to exceed the limits established by the legislature; and that funds intended for the state treasury had been directly appropriated. A hastily organized investigation ordered by the legislature found little basis for most of the charges, though the committee admitted that the actions of the trio had been at times a bit overambitious. They went so far as to point out that the legislature was partially to blame in not having authorized sufficient funds for state buildings and that the personal lot purchases were intended simply to show faith rather than to serve as land speculation. Though serious questions were raised at this point, the voters reelected Governor Butler for a third term.

Edward Rosewater, editor of the Omaha *Bee* and perhaps the most vocal critic of the governor and his party, charged that the entire capital removal was illegal. The legislature rose to the charges, and in 1871, twelve articles of impeachment were drawn and brought against the governor, with similar articles of impeachment delivered to State Auditor Gillespie. Gillespie was exonerated, and 11 of the articles against Butler were dismissed. On the 12th article, as drawn by Mr. Rosewater, Governor Butler was found guilty of making personal use of federal funds intended for the state treasury, and he was ordered removed from office. The result, though temporary, caused a slump in Lincoln's growth and effected a real-estate recession which, coupled with a local drought, nationwide depression, and subsequent grasshopper attacks, plagued the city's prosperity until 1876.

Charles Gere, as Mr. Butler's private secretary, member of the state legislature, and editor of the *Nebraska State Journal*, was uniquely situated to comment on Mr. Butler's actions. Looking back years later, he recalled:

The founders of Lincoln had to fight every inch of the way, under fire from open opponents and pretended friends. They deliberately violated the law which required them to pay the proceeds of Lincoln lots into the state treasury, for they found that the money once there would be tied up by adverse law suits and they would have no funds to pay for the public buildings. They acquired the habit of doing things with a high hand. Their own personal credit was pledged to make the new capital city a success. They had induced many friends to invest. Their plans required large amounts of ready cash. They took the risk of "borrowing" state funds to attain the objective set before them—the creation of a capital city and railroad center on the raw prairie. They believed they could put the project

Above: The Lincoln Electric Lighting Plant facility in Lincoln is shown around the turn of the century. This first plant was originally a part of the Lincoln Street Railway system, which generated electric power to supply its streetcars and sold the excess to consumers.

Top: In order to accommodate people who had purchased railroad land, the Burlington operated this emigrant house north of the depot. Here land buyers could unload their belongings and livestock and prepare to move to their homesteads. Laundry, restaurant, and lodging facilities were maintained for the emigrants' use at a minimum expense.

through in spite of opposition. They did put it through. In the end the state got all its money back, and the new capital became the pride of Nebraska.

David Butler retired to his farm in Pawnee County, was ultimately cleared of wrong-doing by the legislature, was elected to the state senate in 1882 on an independent ticket, and though not elected, was nominated for governor in 1888.

On the heels of Governor Butler's removal, the Omaha *Herald* called for the firing of the University of Nebraska's administrator, John L. McConnell, describing him as one of Butler's "unrepentant henchmen." The university denied the charge, but the constant questions surrounding the staff and the board of regents, and whether the school was following the Morrill Act's provisions left the public with grave misgivings. The predicted enrollment of 300 the second year was tempered by the grasshopper plague and drought, and the term opened with only 123 official students. The next year showed a slip to 100, but the figure rose to 132 the following year and nearly 200 by the beginning of the 1875 term.

Under the terms of the Morrill Land-Grant College Act, which provided federal aid for the establishment of the university, the institution was required to offer an agricultural education. The University of Nebraska College of Agriculture was instituted, at least in name, in 1872, with about 40 acres north of the campus set up as a model farm. This location also housed the hog sheds, which caused a small group of students, loosely organized by Roscoe Pound, to argue against the proximity of the farm, particularly when the wind was northerly. To make his point, Pound (later dean of the Nebraska and Harvard law schools) fired the ROTC cannon, charged with broken brick, into the hog pens, producing a sizable quantity of kindling and bacon. The point was made. In 1874 the regents sold the farmland and purchased the 320-acre Moses Culver farm northeast of the city. This became the campus of the

College of Agriculture, among arguments over whether it should be a model farm or an experimental farm. The Culver home was supplemented with a frame dormitory, and the university catalog advertised that a "student can {here} find a pleasant home, far enough from the city to be out of the way of its temptations to idleness and worse. Students are required to work at least two hours per day for five days a week at 10-15 cents per hour. Board and room $3 per week."

In 1872 it was not uncommon to find coyotes and deer within the city limits, as the city was rapidly growing into areas that

the wild animal population saw only as potential forage when winter snows covered the prairie grass. As spring approached, animals were a frequent topic at the city council meetings. Another problem faced by a rapidly growing prairie city was fire control. Once a fire started, the frame buildings offered little resistance, and the lack of a piped water supply meant that bucket brigades or tank wagons were the only means of quenching a fire. Also, as the city grew, buildings were becoming larger, requiring an even more plentiful source of water. Part of the answer was found in the purchase of fire pumper wagons, but a source of water to pump was still a very real problem. The proposed solution was to construct a series of large cisterns made of tar-covered timbers, buried under streets, sidewalks, and parks.

When this photo was taken in 1887, Lincoln had nearly 30 dressmakers and milliners. This shop at 132 South 11th Street was probably operated by Mrs. D.G. King at that time.

As the depression of 1873 waited around the corner, an idea was proffered to pay for the needed construction. The city of Omaha had, more or less successfully, issued fiat paper money, or scrip, to finance its share of the building costs for the territorial capitol. The lure of printing local money was irresistible. The device had been in use by cities, banks, firms, and states since 1830. In essence the notes were promises to pay the bearer a stated sum of money when presented. The notes would be issued to the contractor, who would in turn buy supplies and pay his workers with them. So long as the notes continued to circulate, money had literally been created. And since they looked like currency, they would presumably continue to be spent as long as confidence in the solvency of the issuer remained high. In a manner of speaking, they were more like checks with an infinite number of endorsers.

On May 20, 1872, Mayor E.E. Brown, councilmen J.J. Gosper and L.A. Scoggin, and council finance chairman S.G. Owen were authorized to negotiate for the printing of one, two, and three dollar denominations with suitable designs. On August 20 the printing of $10,000 worth of notes was ordered from the Continental Bank Note Company, which subsequently delivered 1,500 sheets of one and two dollar notes to the city treasurer. At this point it was learned that the U.S. government had instituted a 10-percent tax on such issues, that no more than 50 percent of any given project could be so financed, and that outstanding projects could not be paid off with them. With this news, the scrip idea was shelved, and none of the notes was ever signed or issued.

The first things necessary for a community in the Great Plains were a saloon, a bank, an undertaker, and a shoemaker. In 1879 shoemaker W.G. Marshall moved his family from Westernville, Iowa, and set up shop on the north side of O Street near 12th.

The notes were not heard of again until the *Nebraska State Journal* reported on October 16, 1874, that some of the notes had found their way to the federal government for redemption. To prevent this from recurring, the U.S. Secret Service was sent to seek out and destroy any remaining specimens. Again their existence was forgotten until 1894, when the State National Bank was being remodeled and Will Stein found a cache of the notes plastered into a wall. Mr. Stein promptly sold the lot for "eight or ten dollars." Much of it found its way into the hands of Louie Kroner and his clerk W.E. Ludwig, who printed store advertising across the back and gave it away. Within a

Opposite: In 1873 Lincoln's first high school building was completed at 15th and M. One of the first expenditures was for the trees planted around the block to protect the building from prairie fires.

Above: The Lincoln High School class of 1888 is shown posing on January 17, 1887.

few weeks the bills had been scattered over the entire Midwest and occasionally passed as legitimate money. The Secret Service frowned on this unofficial currency and once again attempted to destroy all the extant specimens. Today probably fewer than 25 or 30 of each denomination still exist, in the hands of collectors— interesting, if worthless (except to numismatists), reminders of Lincoln's attempt to print its own money.

With the economy of the area suffering and the city investigating unorthodox methods of raising revenue, it was hardly the most asupicious time to propose a $50,000 bond issue to build a new high school, but by 1871 the school-age population had reached 713, and facilities were

severely strained. After Mr. and Mrs. Merrill's dirt-floored classroom in the old seminary burned in 1867, the citizens held fund-raising events to build a small stone building on the northeast corner of 11th and Q, where 35 students were taught for a fee of 50 cents a month. When attendance reached 65, the old Methodist church on the southwest corner of 10th and Q was purchased as an annex. A third school, known as the "South School" and later the "J Street School," on the northeast corner of 8th and J, was soon also added.

The bond issue was passed by the electorate in 1871, and the voters were then asked to choose one of three sites for the new high school: 15th and M, 15th and G, or 11th and J streets. The 15th and M site won, and in December the plans submitted by Roberts and Boulanger were accepted. In January 1873 the three-story brick and stone high school was opened for 250 students from grades one through twelve, but not without considerable grumbling from the press and public. It was pointed out that the building, which was supposed to be only a high school, was large enough to hold all the high-school students in the state. It was so large that it could never be properly utilized—the voters had been hoodwinked. Moreover, the school board went back to the city council and asked for an additional $50 to purchase a *Webster's Unabridged Dictionary,* a copy of *Lippincott's Gazette,* and a number of evergreen trees. The trees, it was quickly pointed out, were not for shade or decoration. In the parents' haste to locate the school, they had chosen a site so far to the east of the city that a green belt was needed to protect the building from prairie fires. The isolated location was apparently a real obstacle; well into the next decade many parents would not allow their children to walk to school in winter for fear that they might be attacked by wild animals. Eventually, of course, the city expanded, and the school-age population continued to grow—to 1,313 in 1875, 2,832 in 1880, and 4,421 in 1890.

The first post office in the Lincoln vicinity was operated by John J. Gregory,

Jr., who was appointed postmaster for Gregory's Basin, near the present West Lincoln, on May 28, 1863. With the establishment of Lancaster County, Jacob Dawson became the village of Lancaster's postmaster on September 15, 1864, when about 20 people constituted the entire population. The salary for the office was seven dollars a year. On the positive side of the job was the fact that the small amount of mail arrived only once a month. On the negative side was the problem that Mr. Dawson had to ride to Yankee Hill to get the mail from the federal supply wagons headed to Fort Kearny. Because of this inconvenience, Dawson applied for and was granted a raise of five dollars a year. Like other small post offices, the postmaster's home was the official office, but the mail was usually on the person of Mr. Dawson. Thus the first home within Lancaster's boundaries was also the first post office. When Lincoln became the state capital, and the population jumped from 30 in 1867 to 800 the following year, the federal government increased the deliveries to once a week, now coming directly to Lincoln on the overland stage. This meant that Mr. Dawson's work was likewise increased, and again he applied for a raise. This time the increase was denied, and Mr. Dawson quit.

Through the next few years the post office was kept in private homes and rented or donated shops, including the old Hallo Opera House on the southwest corner of 12th and O streets. In 1871 Senator John M. Thayer began lobbying for a post office/U.S. customhouse/federal courthouse for Lincoln. It was not until 1873, however, that the federal government actually announced its intention to build. A team of investigators toured the city and reported that the best site was in block 43, located between O and P and 9th and 10th streets. This site was their first choice because it was vacant, had the highest elevation in the city, from which the "rim of the prairie" was visible in all directions, and was already publicly owned, having been deeded to the city by the state in 1867 for use as a haymarket square. On

March 31, 1873, Governor Robert W. Burns authorized the city to sell the property to the federal government, provided that a new haymarket was established. To this end the city purchased property east of the capitol building. This they gave to the State Historical Society in exchange for the block bounded by 9th, 10th, Q, and R streets, which became the new market area. On April 1, 1873, the O Street property was deeded to the U.S. government. The site survey was completed on May 25, 1874, and the following day an official ground breaking was held.

As had been the case with other government contracts, suitable building materials were difficult to obtain, but finally the supervising architect, Alfred B. Mullett, gave his approval to native Nebraska limestone quarried at the Gwyer Quarries near Plattsmouth. The High Victorian Gothic post office was completed in 1879 at a cost of more than $200,000.

As a part of the land transfer, the federal government also agreed to "drill

This 1882 photo shows a livery stable on the west side of South 13th Street near N Street. Frank Rawlings is shown holding the horse; the man standing near the pump is M.L. Rawlings.

and maintain in perpetuity" a well on the grounds. In 1875 this well was sunk and provided a saline artesian flow to a stone fountain directly north of the building. It was said that anything that tasted so bad had to be good for you, and the water was instantly reputed to cure arthritis and practically any ailment known to humanity. Water was carried away in tin cups, pails, and jars. An interesting sidelight is that while the well was being drilled, progress was halted for several days while the U.S.

Assay Office sent investigators to check on the discovery of a small vein of gold more than 100 feet below the city. The gold was real but small in quantity, and the government was more interested in a post office than a gold mine. Although it was much discussed for a time, it was soon forgotten.

As if the times were not bad enough, the Hallo Opera House, which had been the city's only real entertainment center since it was built in 1869, burned to the ground in 1875 after a production of "The Two Orphans." Despite the economic conditions, a public subscription that year raised more than $9,000 to build a new theater, which was completed in 1876 and appropriately named the Centennial Opera House. The opera house, though economically successful, was physically a bit precarious. The sidewalk just west of the building became a bridge, as a usually dry creek bed crossed O Street on a diagonal and drained a spring-fed swamp at about 14th and P streets. When the spring rains came, O Street at 12th was nearly impassable, with planks laid on the mud to assist brave pedestrians.

As the downtown was crisscrossed with arroyos and dry stream beds, paving projects were begun in the 1880s, beginning with the problem area at 11th and P, which was paved with long-lasting cedar blocks set in sand, much as brick would later be employed. In 1889 five-and-a-half miles of the city's 200 miles of streets were paved, and seven additional miles were paved the following year.

On November 15, 1875, a meeting was announced for Lincoln's old stone schoolhouse on the northeast corner of 11th and Q. The topic of discussion was the possible merger of the Young Men's Library and Lecture Association and the Ladies' Library and Reading Room Association. The result of the merger was the Lincoln Public Library and Reading Room Association, the forerunner of the present Lincoln public library system. The minutes show that Prosper Smith, in order to encourage further gifts, donated a complete set of *Appleton's American*

Schwab's store near 11th and O offered men's and boys' clothing. Today the site is occupied by Gold's Galleria.

Above: The Nebraska State Capitol building is seen in the late 1800s.

Opposite: By the mid-1890s much of Lincoln's streetcar system was powered with electricity, which meant a great maze of overhead wires. Here a Lincoln Street Railway Company car is shown in front of the county courthouse at 10th and K streets. When first completed, the courthouse building had a "copper" statue of Abraham Lincoln atop the tower. The statue was removed when it was found to be deteriorating—not made of copper. The presence of the statue dates this photo before 1900.

Encyclopedia. The treasurer's report showed funds of $984, with a total of 12 life members and 130 annual members.

The new library opened for business on January 28, 1876, with Ada Van Pelt on duty. Because there was such a small treasury, the board members served as librarian on a rotational basis until a paid employee was finally hired in 1882. The day the library opened, its shelves contained 376 books. In 1877 the library received its first funding from the city, $100, given at the direction of Mayor H.W. Hardy. Things got tougher shortly afterward, and it was necessary to charge a dollar a year membership for a time. The library moved from rented room to rented room until 1898, when it occupied the second floor of the Masonic Temple at 11th and M.

On September 16, 1899, a disastrous fire, which saw the end of the city's volunteer fire department, destroyed the library and several other buildings. It was said that the librarian calculated the number of volumes checked out that night to determine how many books the library owned after the fire. The number was 376—the same number it had owned on opening day! Mary Baird Bryan, William Jennings Bryan's wife, contacted Andrew Carnegie, who gave $75,000 and later another $2,000 for the construction of a new building to

be located on the northeast corner of 14th and N. The new Carnegie Library was occupied on May 27, 1902, with a shelf capacity of 33,000 volumes. By 1916 more than 40,000 volumes were in the collection, and in 1937 the collection numbered 110,000 volumes, underscoring the great need for the new Bennett Martin Public Library, which was opened on the same site on October 17, 1962.

By 1876 the economic depression was over at last, and a period of renewed growth began. The political center of the state was rapidly becoming a transportation center, with four major railway systems and several connecting lines radiating in all directions. The Burlington and Missouri River Railroad owned 42 miles of switching track, employed 800 yard employees, and had 13 passenger and 58 freight trains operating daily in 1889. All forms of commerce and manufacturing prospered— except for the salt business. What many had hoped would provide the capital with an economic basis was finally given up as impractical.

The central focus of Lincoln's growth and existence had always been the capitol building, but in 1875 the structure was in jeopardy. The governor was forced to issue a proclamation to the senate stating that no matter how stirred they might be by the speeches of their colleagues, under no

Above: W.H. Tyler was responsible for the stonework on the U.S. Post Office/old city hall and on many other early masonry buildings. This photo, taken around 1885, shows his stoneworks at 7th and L.

Top: Even though electricity modernized most of Lincoln's street railway system before the turn of the century, the old horse and mule cars continued to run until 1906. Mayor Frank Zehrung is shown on the last run of the Lyman Street Railway system.

circumstances were they to applaud or stamp their feet. The building was literally crumbling beneath them. This gave impetus to a new crop of removalists, who urged that a new city farther west be chosen and a new capitol erected there, closer to the new center of population. Nearly a dozen communities joined the running—the most energetic were Columbus, Clarks, and Kearney—but infighting defeated any chance of removal. In 1879 the state legislature passed an appropriation for a three-story wing to be built west of the existing structure. This was completed and occupied in 1882. Everyone agreed that the wing over-shadowed the original building; the result was an immediate appropriation for an east wing. The plan was to ultimately remove the central building and incorporate the wings into a thoroughly modern building. In 1883 the state accepted W.H.B. Stout's bid to complete the central section of the building at a cost of just under $500,000, while J.S. Gregory paid the state $300 for salvage rights to the old building. The $300 may have been too much, as by 1925 the only known remaining pieces of the first building were the front door, which was on a barn near Weeping Water, and the black wooden ball from the cupola and the front door key, which were in the State Historical Society's archives. In 1888, scarcely 20 years after the first building had been completed, the state had built its

second capitol, and the last active removal cries were finally squelched.

In 1867 the state set aside a square block of land in the capital city's plat for the use of the county, but with only limited funds available the county decided to rent the second floor of Lincoln's first bank, the Sweet and Brock Bank, on the northeast corner of 10th and O. When the lease was renewed two years later, a group of citizens petitioned the county commissioners to poll the voters on the advisability of issuing $50,000 in bonds for the construction of a courthouse and jail. Although the bond issue was not on the ballot, the county was authorized to transfer several blocks of land to the state in exchange for the block at 10th and J, to be used as the ultimate site of a county courthouse. In 1882 the commissioners decided to put the question of a five-year, five-mill levy on property in the county to raise $125,000 for courthouse construction; meanwhile the county bought a small two-story frame building on the southeast corner of 9th and R for $800. It was not until 1887 that the question actually made the ballot, at which time the voters approved a $200,000 bond issue.

That summer the board toured courthouses in five states and asked for plans from seven architects. In July the plan of E.E. Myers and Son of Detroit was chosen, but bids on the design ranged from $270,000 to $330,000. A second round of bids proved just as high. New plans were solicited, and this time the architectural firm of F.M. Ellis of Omaha was chosen. W.H.B. Stout of Lincoln was awarded the construction contract for $168,000. Finally completed in 1890, the result proved worth the wait. Some even felt that it put the new capitol in second place and was one of the finest buildings in the state. The nearly fireproof structure was made of Berea, Ohio, sandstone, brick, tile, and slate. The tower was topped with what was purported to be a copper statue of Abraham Lincoln. When deterioration caused the removal of the tower, it was discovered that the statue was made of lead sheathing, not copper, and had virtually dissolved.

As Lincoln grew and became a real city, demands for utilities caused government and private business to offer more and more metropolitan advantages. The demand for paving of the downtown area

After locating in a number of rented homes and suffering a disastrous fire in 1889, Lincoln's library finally got a proper building in 1903, with a great deal of help from Andrew Carnegie. The building stood on the northeast corner of 14th and N, the site of the present Bennett Martin Public Library.

Above: After the state purchased the old Lancaster County Fairgrounds for use as a location for the state fair, a number of permanent buildings were erected. One of the first was Agricultural Hall, shown here at the turn of the century.

Top: One area of Agricultural Hall at the state fair was used for the county agronomy competition. This photo shows a portion of the Nemaha County exhibit.

brought about the realization that storm and sanitary sewers should be installed first; it was also noted that that was the economical time to install sidewalks. Thus the appearance of Lincoln's downtown was transformed, virtually overnight, into an area "as beautiful as any place of its age in the United States," according to the *Agents Bulletin* of the Missouri Pacific Iron Mountain Company.

The Lincoln Street Railway was incorporated in 1870 by J.D. MacFarland but was forced to wait until 1881 to be voted a right-of-way on the city streets. After a brief trial, to make sure the horse-drawn cars could climb the hill from the depot, Joe Herrich paid his nickel in 1883 and became the city's first streetcar passenger. Later that same year there were 37 cars using 200 horses and operating on 18 miles of track. There were brief experiments with steam, compressed air, and cables in various cities, but in 1891 Lincoln's streetcar line became one of the first in the United States to begin conversion to electricity. This brought about the merger of several smaller lines to form the new Lincoln Street Railway Company. Because the company produced electricity in excess of its needs, a few private power customers were accommodated, making it the first electric company in the city as well.

For seven years the first city water well, sunk in 1882 in Lincoln Park at 7th and F, supplied more than a million gallons of water daily. By 1887 this supply was being taxed. Attempts to enlarge it by drilling supplemental wells in 6th Street produced only salt water. In 1889 a well in the Antelope Creek watershed at 23rd and N began adding another million gallons a day and was later joined by scores of wells along the creek's channel to the south. In 1872 the Lincoln Gas Light Company began manufacturing producer gas, and in 1886 gas streetlights were introduced.

In 1877 Louis Korty and J.J. Dickey of Omaha secured a franchise from the Bell Telephone Company for parts of Nebraska and Iowa. Several two-party lines were established in Lincoln, but an exchange

was not built until 1880 when 65 subscribers were interconnected through the
telephone offices in the Holmes Block
between 11th and 12th on O Street. By
1889, six hundred and fifteen subscribers
could not only call each other but could
also be connected with 57 Nebraska and 66
Iowa towns. In 1895 Nebraska Bell built a
new three-story exchange on 13th Street,
just south of the alley between O and N
streets, to serve its 800 customers.

The first fair to be held in Lincoln was
the Lancaster County exhibit, which opened on October 13, 1870. The first territorial fair in the United States had been held
in Nebraska City beginning on September
21, 1859. State fairs moved from year to
year, hosted in turn by Omaha, Nebraska
City, Brownville, and Lincoln. Under the
leadership of Charles H. Gere and J.D.
MacFarland, the 1899 legislature was
convinced to purchase the Lancaster
County Fairgrounds and there build
a permanent home for the Nebraska
State Fair.

One of the most bizarre and far-reaching
events to take place in Nebraska began as
Lincoln was officially recognized by the
state as a city of the first class on March
25, 1887. Lincoln historian Andrew J.
Sawyer was elected mayor on the reform
platform, and the following were elected to
the city council: Lorenzo W. Billingsley,
Lewis C. Pace, Granville Ensign, William J.
Cooper, Joseph Z. Briscoe, James Dailey,
John Fraas, Robert B. Graham, Henry H.
Dean, Fred A. Hovey, John M. Burks, and
Nelson C. Brock. Elected the previous year
and with one year left to serve was Police
Judge Albert F. Parsons. In August a group
of gamblers filed a complaint with the city
council charging Parsons with pocketing
fine money rather than turning it over to
the county treasurer. It was soon uncovered that Parsons had, under the guise
of a Nebraska statute, fined certain
gamblers and madames $10 a month plus
five dollars a month per employee. In
order to expedite justice he did not require
the parties to appear in court; he simply
visited their premises and directly pocketed
the fines. This meant that there were no

A pool room in the city
of Havelock shows that
area residents enjoyed
"corrupt" forms of
entertainment as much as
their Eastern
counterparts did. J.B.
Headrick (great-grandfather
of this book's author)
built this and several
other buildings in the
city of Havelock, now a
suburban area in
northeast Lincoln.

J.H. Harley at center emigrated from Nova Scotia to Lincoln, opening his drug- and bookstore on the southeast corner of 11th and O about 1876.

warrants, arrests, or written evidence. An investigative committee recommended to the full council that the mayor be informed and that the office of police judge be declared vacant and a replacement appointed.

Here the incident would ordinarily have been closed. But Mr. Parsons was considerably irritated at losing such a lucrative position. Mr. Parsons' attorney approached the U.S. circuit court judge in St. Louis and asked for an order to restrain the council from firing the judge. The claim was that his client had been deprived of his constitutional rights without due process of law. The judge agreed, issued the restraining order, and ordered the defendants to appear in court in Omaha on October 24, 1887.

The council's legal advice was that the federal court had no jurisdiction over their actions, and they continued with their "trial" of Mr. Parsons. The committee's suggestion was upheld, and Mayor Sawyer instructed the marshal to physically remove Mr. Parsons and install H.J. Whitmore in the vacant office. Ex-judge Parsons promptly complained to the circuit court, which ordered the mayor and council to appear in Omaha on November 15 to answer federal charges of contempt. Warrants were issued and served. At the appointed hour Judges Elmer S. Dundee and David J. Brewer called upon Mr. G.M. Lambertson, counsel to the council and mayor, to show cause why they should not be found guilty of contempt. After both sides had spoken, Councilman Ensign was so confident of the outcome that he personally offered to pay any fines levied against them. Following a rather dramatic speech, the lot was found guilty. Briscoe, Burks, and Cooper were fined only $50 each, as they had been opposed to the proceedings in question. The other eight were fined $600 each plus court costs. Mr. Ensign had a total of $10.13 cash with him.

Mr. Lambertson boarded a train for Washington, D.C., to obtain a writ of habeas corpus from the U.S. Supreme Court, and the prisoners were marched to jail. Along the way Councilman Dean received permission to stop in a drugstore to fill his prescription for "alcohol" and afterward carried a bag that audibly clinked all the way to prison. Here they were put up in two rooms that were the living quarters of the deputy sheriff. Councilman Burks produced a letter from his doctor and $50 cash and bought his freedom, leaving the rest to wait out their sentences. In the days that followed they were visited by judges, senators, and various well-wishers, including J. Sterling Morton and Governor Thayer, who promised to visit the President personally if necessary to secure their pardon if they were not exonerated. Cigars, flowers, and gifts flowed in so quickly that a commissary had to be established. A free telegraph station was opened for the prisoners' use, and they were allowed to dine out, attend plays, and go to church services while technically confined.

After six days the U.S. Attorney General, who was astounded that the group was actually in jail, ordered the prisoners released to their homes in custody of Deputy United States Marshal Allen. Their return to Lincoln was attended by the police and fire departments, a Knights of Pythias lodge parade, and a band, and marked by speeches from General Webster and other dignitaries. Governor Thayer produced a petition signed by himself, numerous judges, state officials, attorneys, and others and again promised to deliver the list to the President if necessary. On December 12, 1887, the case was heard by the U.S. Supreme Court, while Governor Thayer met with President Cleveland. The President commented that "they do seem to be standing for a sound democratic principle—the doctrine of home rule. It is a principle that ought to be triumphant." Finally on January 10, 1888, the court, eagerly watched by municipalities, counties, and states nationwide, issued its verdict, stating that the lower court had acted without jurisdiction. The mayor and council were vindicated—the principle of home rule was officially the law of the land.

CHAPTER V

THE CITY EXPANDS

As the turn of the century approached, the village of Lincoln was fast becoming an urban center of transportation, commerce, government, and education. Since becoming the second-largest city in the state, surpassing Nebraska City in 1875, its growth had been relatively steady with only a short period of falling population in the 1890s.

Nebraska Bell Telephone was in the forefront of the city's commercial growth as it moved into its new home at 130 South 13th Street (now the site of a restaurant appropriately called the Exchange) in 1895. At the open house visitors were awed by a floral arrangement with a concealed telephone that delivered musical entertainment originating in the manager's home and later from a group performing in Omaha. In 1897 a connection was completed to Chicago. Lincoln's 1,500 subscribers could now hold a five-minute conversation with the "windy city" for a mere $5.50.

As the 17-year Bell Company patents on the original telephone began to expire in 1893, local entrepreneurs quickly moved to fill the voids left by Bell in rural areas and its general failure to keep its equipment current with such new technology as the dial telephone. In May 1900 the Western Independent Long Distance Telephone Company of Plattsmouth received permission to operate in Lincoln. Mayor H.J. Winnett promptly vetoed the authorization, but on March 9, 1903, he signed a franchise for the Western Union Independent Telephone Company, which had been incorporated two days earlier by

Frank H. Woods, Charles J. Bills, and Judge Allen Field. In just over a year the company, now renamed the Lincoln Telephone Company, began service with nearly 2,000 subscribers. Because there was no interconnection between the two companies, doctors and enterprising merchants had to have two separate phones so that they could receive calls from or reach subscribers of either company. As often happens, competition brought a price war, with Bell offering a reduced rate and a 25-year contract in order to sink its independent rival.

Bell's sheer size was then brought into play, in conjunction with the economic panic of 1907. Many independent companies with their far from adequate capitalization were simply unable to weather the period and were forced into bankruptcy. Lincoln Telephone was forced to raise its rates at the same time as Bell moved to lower its by 50 cents a month, and the independent suddenly lost 20 percent of its subscribers. By 1910 what was known as the "Great Bell War" had begun in earnest. As president of the National Independent Telephone Association, Frank Woods became the spokesman in the negotiations that ensued regarding antitrust laws, utility regulation, and so-called watered stock sales. A vast plan was proposed involving some mergers of independent firms with Bell, strengthening some independents by buying out conflicting Bell interests, establishing toll agreements, and dividing certain territories. Under this agreement Lincoln Telephone

The Burlington "hump" west of Lincoln was an artificial hill utilized to make up trains, using a gravity-sorting system. This crew at the hump is shown about 1915. The old steel and wood bridge over the sorting tracks was a popular stop for sightseers from the 1920s through the 1960s. In 1983 the gravity hump area was closed; diesel engines are now used to sort cars and make up trains.

Above: The first O Street viaduct was built as a joint venture by the city and railroad, although both constantly argued over whose responsibility maintenance and upkeep should be.

Top: Horse fountains were a frequent traffic obstacle in Lincoln's wholesale district. This one, given by the U.S. Humane Society, was in the middle of M Street between 8th and 9th.

Opposite page, top: In 1906 Castle, Roper & Matthews introduced the first horse-drawn ambulance in Lincoln, and in 1912 the firm owned the city's first automobile hearse and ambulance. The building at 1319 N survived until the 1970s, when it was razed for a parking lot. The Roper & Sons' building at 4300 O Street became their central mortuary.

and Telegraph, recently merged with the Western Telephone Company, purchased Bell interests in 22 southeast Nebraska counties, and Nebraska Bell purchased LT&T interests outside the outlined areas, primarily those north of the Platte River. The agreement was concluded on January 22, 1912, with the issuance of a check from LT&T to Nebraska Telephone Company for $2,293,000—the largest check ever issued, up to that time, in Lancaster County. From then on the 1,211 subscribers who had maintained two separate telephones were able to communicate with the city's other 13,500 phones on one instrument. At the same time the now greatly enlarged firm announced construction of a three-story building at 14th and M, a block south and a block east of the original 1903 structure, and added a number of employee benefits formerly unheard of, such as vacations and sick leave.

Unless one considers Yankee Hill (which originated at about the same time as Lancaster) a suburb, then Lincoln's first suburb was University Place. The site was originally known as Athens, so named by the first postmaster, W. Gage Miller, on February 12, 1889. At about the same time the local Methodist Episcopal bishop appointed a commission to determine how the church's two schools at York and Central City might be strengthened. The commission's plan called for building a major new college, with the two existing schools being subordinate to it and providing classes only up to the sophomore level. To this end 44 acres were purchased northeast of Lincoln at Athens. On July 30, 1889, Athens became University Place and was officially incorporated. The church commission had pledged $50,000 for the construction of the school, but the lot sales proceeded so well that an additional expenditure of $20,000 was authorized. Architects Gibbs and Parker of Kansas City planned the thoroughly modern structure—"compactly built, with few projections and almost no towers...a solid building three stories high of pressed brick and red stone, the only embellishment being a clock tower

reaching about 30 feet, fronting the setting sun." Work progressed well. The cornerstone was laid on September 22, 1887, and the doors were opened to both male and female students at $10 a term on September 25. The one building, like University Hall at the state university, housed the entire school: 30 classrooms, chemistry laboratories, a 1,000-seat chapel, a library, offices, manual training areas, and a museum. Contrary to the experience of many other Midwestern universities, Nebraska Wesleyan and its city grew, and by the fall of 1888 enough houses had been constructed to quarter all the female students.

A second suburb, Havelock, began life as the village of Newton. It was originally settled by George G. Smith, W.J. Johnson, O. Master, and Dr. J.A. Scott, each of

Left: Harvey W. Hardy moved to the village of Lincoln in 1871 when the population was less than 2,500. His first store, at 800 O Street, was a great success and became the first of many as the Hardy Furniture Company moved to larger quarters through the years. The company closed in January 1973, on the day of the store's 101st anniversary. This Hardy's delivery truck loaded with mattresses was photographed circa 1900.

Havelock's main street was known as Jackson Street and later O Street, before the city was annexed to Lincoln in 1930 and the street name became Havelock Avenue. In this 1900 photo we are looking east through Havelock's business district with the Lincoln/Havelock car in the foreground.

whom built a small frame building in the late 1880s. The location several miles northeast of Lincoln was almost accidentally located near the right-of-way of the Burlington and Missouri River Railroad, but fate was not going to let Newton exist very long as a "whistle stop with a train to Lincoln available every 20 minutes." A.E. Touzalin formed a partnership with two other Burlington land agents and bought a 200-acre farmstead near Newton from Elder Miller and as many other smaller tracts as they could round up, forming the Lancaster Land Company. They then offered a goodly portion of the tract to the Burlington, free of charge, if it would establish on the land a shop to serve the railroad's western division. The city of Plattsmouth, only about 50 miles east, had just completed eight large buildings for a division machine shop employing more than 500 men, and for a time it seemed likely that the Newton shops would be considered too close to the existing facility. Although the reasoning is unclear, the Burlington accepted the proposition, and by June of 1890 the construction of a 130- by 400-foot machine

shop was under way. On May 6, 1893, the town was incorporated, with its name changed to Havelock in honor of Mr. Touzalin's idol, English General John Havelock. By 1910 the Burlington had spent $2.5 million on the buildings, and the labor force was well over 500. In 1913 the city boasted two weekly newspapers, two banks, several hotels, and its own gasworks, electric-lighting plant, and telephone exchange, as well as a complete selection of retail and service businesses.

Bethany, like University Place, was created around a denominational school. In 1886 a group of businessmen bought the Hawley farm and several smaller parcels of land east of Lincoln; each partner contributed from 5 to 85 acres to the total tract of 321 acres. They then offered a major portion of the land to the Baptist Church, on condition that the church build a Baptist college on the site. The plan, like many others concocted by speculators, assumed that as the school grew and prospered a support community would grow up around it, making the remaining land considerably more valuable than the original purchase price. Unfortunately, the Baptists felt that their resources were being strained by their existing Nebraska institution, and they rejected the offer. J.Z. Briscoe, representing the Nebraska Christian Missionary Alliance, quickly asked that his group be considered for the land offer. Almost at once the Christian Church was also offered 500 acres of land southwest of Lincoln by a similar investment group. With the inclusion of an additional 18 city lots, said to be worth in excess of $4,000, the eastern package was accepted in 1888. The area was called Bethany Heights in honor of Bethany College in West Virginia, the Christian Church's first university.

On August 30, 1888, a group of nearly 200 people gathered at the Missouri Pacific depot in Lincoln for a trip to Newman's Station (now about 66th and Vine streets). After a three-quarter-mile walk north, they were met by a group of about 50 others who had arrived by wagon for a picnic in a small grove and the official cornerstone laying for Nebraska Christian University. An auction of city lots was held to raise construction funds, and $8,315 worth of the $100 to $400 lots were sold the first day. O.C. Placey's design for a building to cost $85,000 was chosen, and while classes started in 1889 in the Demarest home, construction began. The five-story stone and brick building, built by Thomas Price, contained 32 classrooms, 7 offices, a 500-seat chapel, a library, and a study hall. At the first commencement in 1890 spirits were high, and it was predicted that by 1924 eight additional buildings would be needed. On November 10, 1890, the village of Bethany was officially incorporated. A gymnasium was built in 1907, and a short time later a 16-room women's dormitory was built at a cost of $4,373. Unfortunately, the school found itself in financial trouble almost from the opening day. Samuel Cotner, one of many benefactors over the course of the school's lifetime, donated more than 50 acres of land, helping to save the school during one of its acute financial crises, and the school was renamed Cotner College in his honor.

One of the smaller suburbs of Lincoln

A common sight in 1920s Lincoln was the knife and scissors sharpener, who went from door to door in search of work.

was never incorporated and never even had a post office, but Normal did have a bank, several retail businesses, and a famous national figure as a resident— William Jennings Bryan. In 1891 J.F. Saylor of Shenandoah, Iowa, undertook the establishment of a private "normal school" in a new development about three miles southeast of Lincoln. The area was named Normal, after the school, by its developers, E.R. Sizer, who later became the college's business manager, and John H. McClay. The area covered the land bounded now by 48th, 56th, A, and Calvert streets. The main building, designed by Artemus Roberts, used $86,000 of the promoters' total capital outlay of $300,000. The school, which opened in September 1892, reported an enrollment of 575 by the second term. Two popular features were that classes could be started at any time, and board, room, and tuition for an eight-week session cost only $24. At its opening one reporter suggested that the building was built to "stand the wear and tear of centuries." Unfortunately, the author did not reckon on a fire in 1898, which virtually destroyed the main building and closed the institution. The property was purchased by Dr. Benjamin F. Bailey, who converted the former girls' dormitory and dining room into a sanitarium and in 1901 greatly expanded the facility with the addition of a new main building.

The community of College View, like Bethany and University Place, began around a denominational college. The first Seventh-Day Adventist attempt at higher education in the Midwest began in a church basement in Minneapolis with 100 badly crowded students. In 1889 the church decided to establish a college on the Great Plains. When church officials visited Lincoln, a group of local businessmen offered them 300 acres of land, consisting mainly of corn and sunflower fields, southeast of the city. The committee was favorably impressed by the community and the several institutions of higher learning already in existence, and the offer was accepted. The church authorized $100,000 for construction, and in 1890 ground was

broken for College Hall.

One of the first residents of the new community was W.C. Sisley, who was chosen to be the architect and builder of the school's physical plant. As soon as he arrived, Mr. Sisley erected a large barn just north of 48th and Prescott (named for W.W. Prescott, first president of Union College), where the first church services in the community were held. Shortly afterward Zelman Nicola built a two-story general store on the southwest corner of 48th and Prescott. Classes began in 1891, and on April 28, 1892, the village was incorporated.

The first few years were difficult, but the town and Union College continued to grow and strengthen. In 1895 Dr. J.D.

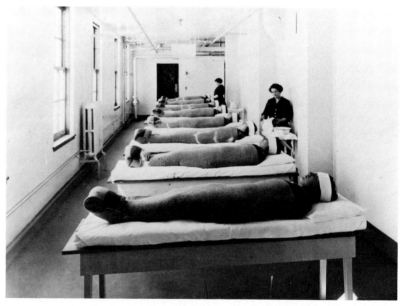

Shively opened the church-related Nebraska Sanitarium in half of one of the dormitories. Within a short time the sanitarium was flourishing, while the school continued to suffer declining enrollments, resulting in a 25-year lease on the dormitory to the hospital. As the hard times subsided, the school again needed the dormitory space, and for a time the two church-owned institutions were rivals over the dormitory/sanitarium. The hospital subleased a portion of the building back to the school, then in 1905 bought North Hall, forcing the male students to board in

Opposite: Although Lincoln's State Hospital for the Insane was intended as an insane asylum, its staff was prepared for any medical emergency, as evidenced by this 1914 view of an operating room. Below, nurses attend a lecture at the State Hospital.

Above: Some of the more violent inmates of the State Hospital were treated by extreme confinement, as pictured. The practice was short-lived.

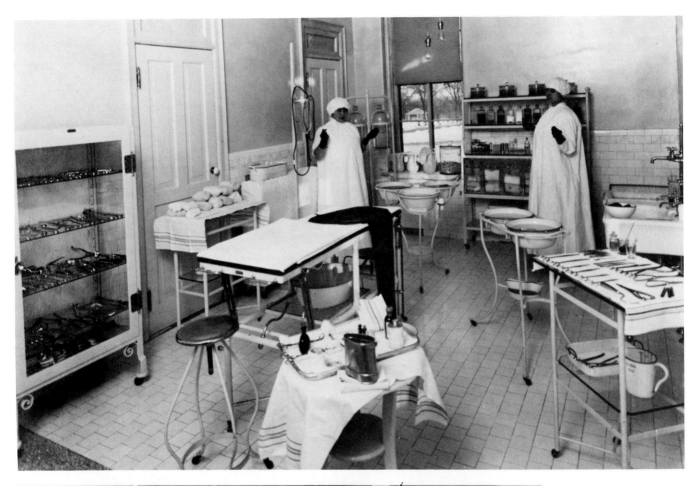

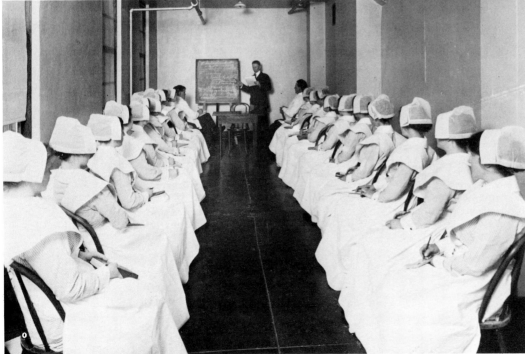

Above: After 1906
Burlington Beach was
known as Capital Beach.
Although the lake
remained an attraction, a
saltwater swimming pool,
dance pavilion, and
midway were far more
popular with the
weekend crowds, which
often numbered in the
thousands.

Top: The damming of
Oak Creek near the
right-of-way of the
Burlington and Missouri
River Railroad created a
popular weekend resort
for Lincolnites. This
view, taken about 1897,
shows what became of
the original Lancaster salt
flats by the time the area
was known as Burlington
Beach.

the school barn and various basements and
attics. A frequent visitor to the campus was
Dr. J.H. Kellogg, originator of cornflakes,
who advocated, among other things, the
peanut as a source of protein in preference
to meat. Soon a Sunday tradition began of
taking the Lincoln Traction Company's
trolley out Sheridan Boulevard and buying
sacks of freshly roasted peanuts from local
vendors. As a result, the suburb acquired
the nickname "Peanut Hill."

The suburb of Belmont can be traced
back to a federal land grant issued in 1868
for a proposed Baptist community. Twenty
years later three groups of promoters
decided to capitalize on the slowly rising
elevation north of Lincoln by building a
series of real-estate developments, each
successively higher than its neighbor to the
south and each more exclusive. The first,
called Belmont, stretched from Salt Creek
north to Adams Street. Daniel Moseley
platted the area in 1887 and began
promotion. The second tier, called Lincoln
Heights, began at Adams and ran to
Benton Street. The owners, George Bigelow
and D.L. Brace, likewise began laying out
lots, and Mr. Bigelow built a large towered
home in hopes of attracting Lincoln's
prominent business and professional men.
The highest tract, on the rim of the
prairie, was called Grand View. Near Grand
View, the Episcopal Church erected the
Worthington Military Academy, of stone
and brick. None of the real-estate developments was ever successful, in part
because of periodic Salt Creek flooding,
and the academy's enrollment peaked at
fewer than 50 boys. In June 1898, while the
cadets were on the parade ground, an
explosion in the school's powder magazine
scattered stone and bricks for several
blocks. Although the building was totally
destroyed, no one was seriously injured.

The tiny village of West Lincoln was
also populated early in the area's history,
when John Gregory settled on what would
now be West Charleston Street, in hopes
of making a living gathering salt. The area
acquired a post office as Gregory's Basin
on May 28, 1863, and was incorporated as
West Lincoln on August 24, 1887, with a

population of 450, headed by Mayor W.C. Austin. Although the post office was short-lived, an 1889 business directory listed a creamery, stockyards, and a canning and packing plant, as well as nearly a dozen retail and service firms.

For nearly two decades Lincoln's entertainment center was on the southwest corner of 12th and O, where Henry Hallo erected his first opera house in 1869 and, after its destruction by fire in 1875, his second theater, the Centennial Opera House, later known as the Funke Opera House. In 1891 the Funke was quickly relegated to second place when J.F. Lansing opened the Lansing Theater on the southwest corner of 13th and P. The four-story building of cut stone and brick was imposing by any standard and cost a princely $250,000. The equipment was the finest of its day, and the building was one of the first air-conditioned structures in the Midwest. The cooling was achieved by circulating air over ice and through the theater and adjoining business offices via several hundred registers. The auditorium

could seat nearly 3,000 spectators in the main hall, six balconies, and three tiers of boxes. The lobby, which was separated from the adjoining offices and businesses by 16-inch-thick solid stone walls, was said to be large enough to accommodate a coach and four, entering on 13th Street, completely turning around, and exiting on P Street, without brushing the walls. The surrounding suites held the city library, the Nebraska Dental College, and a number of professional offices, while the basement contained 12 dressing rooms, "bear pits" (for animal acts), a men's smoking room, and a barber shop.

Lincoln, around the turn of the century, provided a number of nationally prominent figures, three of whom were born there and were members of the same family. Stephen B. Pound came from New York to Lincoln in the winter of 1866-1867 and moved into Jacob Dawson's double log cabin at about 7th and O. Pound had been reading law for some months before his arrival and continued his studies in the evenings while operating the village's first

Roscoe Pound, son of Lincoln attorney S.B. Pound, was born in Lincoln in 1870 and attended the University of Nebraska. After teaching at the university and becoming dean of the law college, he became a judge in the state supreme court. Ultimately becoming dean of the Harvard Law School, Pound can easily be considered Lincoln's most illustrious citizen.

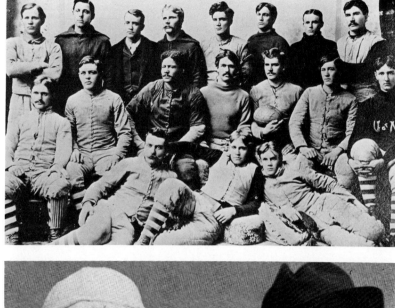

Above: Willa Cather (right) poses with Louise Pound circa 1890. Cather is seen, typically, wearing very short hair and a man's hat. Roscoe Pound's sister Louise went on to become a professor of linguistics, an early folklorist, and the first woman president of the American Folklore Society. Courtesy, Willa Cather Pioneer Memorial Collection, Nebraska State Historical Society

Top: In 1894 the University of Nebraska football team won four of five games. The team defeated Iowa 36-0, Missouri 18-16, Kansas 14-6, and Grinnell 22-0, and lost to Doane 0-12. The player holding the football, team captain George Henry Dern, played right tackle on the early Cornhusker teams of 1893 and 1894. Dern later served as U.S. Secretary of War from 1933 to 1936. Courtesy, University of Nebraska-Lincoln Archives

grocery during the day. On passing the Nebraska Bar, he sold the store to Max Rich and was soon a prominent member of the professional community. In 1870 Stephen's first child, Nathan Roscoe Pound, was born, and by age three he was receiving education from his mother, Laura Biddlecome Pound, who was skeptical of the quality of the local schools. By the time he was six, he began studying German, one of eight foreign languages in which he was to become fluent. Roscoe entered the University of Nebraska at 12, graduated with a degree in biology at 17, and received his doctorate in botany at 18. At 19 he took a one-year law course, passed the Nebraska Bar, and began practicing law in Lincoln. During the next few years he continued his private practice, taught at the university, and began writing. Like his father, he became a judge, but he left the bench to become dean of the Nebraska Law College. In 1916 Pound became dean of the Harvard Law School. He gained international prominence for his writings and his development of a philosophy of law that tempered the old rigid rules of law with the needs of people. His photographic mind and vigorous physical health served him well until his death at age 93, by which time he had become known as the greatest legal scholar in the world.

Louise Pound, Roscoe's sister, was born in 1872 and, like her brother, received her elementary education from her mother. Louise received her A.B. in music from the University of Nebraska in 1892 and earned her master's degree from the same school in 1895. In 1900 the University of Heidelberg in Germany granted her a Ph.D. She joined the University of Nebraska's English faculty in 1894, becoming a full professor in 1912. An accomplished athlete, Louise earned a letter in *men's* tennis, defeated the national and Canadian champions in 1897, became a state golf champion in 1916, and won the Rambler gold medal in 1896 for cycling more than 5,000 miles. In addition she was granted a Litt.D. from Smith College in 1928 and wrote scores of papers and books on

WILLA CATHER: NARRATIVE BEGINNINGS IN LINCOLN

Although Willa Sibert Cather spent only 13 years in Nebraska, and only five of those in Lincoln, she is still virtually always referred to as a Nebraska author. Willa was born to Charles F. and Mary V. Cather on December 7, 1873, though she later claimed the year was 1876. When Willa was nine her family moved from Winchester, Virginia, to Catherton Precinct, Webster County. The area was named for her uncle George P. Cather, who operated a post office under that name for a little more than a year. In less than a year they relocated to Red Cloud, the county seat, where her father operated a quasi-bank. A few years later Mr. Cather purchased the Red Cloud *Republican Chief* and made Willa, then 15, the editor and business manager.

In the fall of 1890 Willa moved to Lincoln, where she roomed with Kate Hastings and a family friend while attending the Latin School of the University of Nebraska. The following year she enrolled at the university. Willa was at once branded an eccentric and a bit of a rebel by some of her classmates: She had her hair cut in man's fashion and occasionally sported men's clothing. As a child she had been an intense reader, so it was natural that her interests soon centered around literature and writing. While still in her freshman year, one of Willa's English professors was so impressed with one of her essays that he submitted it to the Lincoln *Journal*. This was the first time her name had appeared in print.

In 1893 Willa Cather began writing a regular column for the newspaper for one dollar a day, under the titles "One Way of Putting It," "As You Like It," and "The Passing Show." In 1894 she became the *Journal*'s drama critic and found time to contribute fiction to the university *Hesperian*. Under the collected title of *Pastels in Prose*, she wrote *Peter* (later referred to in *My Antonia*) and *Elopement of Allen Poole*. During her university days, her closest friends were Mariel Gere, daughter of the *Journal*'s editor, Charles Gere; Dorothy Canfield, daughter of Chancellor James H. Canfield; and Louise Pound, with whom she co-edited the university *Lasso*.

In 1894 Dorothy suggested the idea for a short story in which the hero is accidentally killed during a football game and his spirit returns to spur the home team's victory. The idea became a story, named "The Fear That Walks by Noonday," and was printed in the university's 1895 annual *Sombrero*. Dorothy and Willa were listed as coauthors, their story won a $10 prize, and it was reprinted in the *Journal*. While at the *Journal*, Cather met and interviewed Stephen Crane and, although one English professor warned that she would never get anywhere as a writer, she began serious consideration of a literary career.

After two years with the *Journal* Willa joined the staff of the Lincoln *Courier*, a society, art, and literary paper, as associate editor. Upon receiving her bachelor of arts degree in 1895, she remained with the *Courier* a few months longer before moving to Pittsburgh. There she worked for the Pittsburgh *Home Monthly*, a competitor of the *Ladies' Home Journal*; and until 1900, Willa continued to send columns, more or less regularly, to the *Courier*.

Her writing and editing careers took her to the Pittsburgh *Daily Leader* (1898-1901) and then to *McClure's Magazine* (1906-1912), where she was the associate editor. In 1917 she published *My Antonia*, which is partially set in Lincoln; and from the University of Nebraska Willa received an honorary bachelor of letters degree, the first of eight degrees she would ultimately receive from various universities. In 1922 her *One of Ours* received the Pulitzer Prize for the best novel of the year. In 1938 she was admitted to the American Academy of Arts and Letters and won its gold medal in 1944. Willa Cather died in New York on April 24, 1947.

Willa Cather is shown on the University of Nebraska campus about 1894. Courtesy, Willa Cather Pioneer Memorial Collection, Nebraska State Historical Society

*During his first campaign
for the U.S. Presidency
in 1896, William Jennings
Bryan devised a novel
way of talking directly to
large numbers of people.
His special train would
stop at virtually every
station, and Bryan would
address as many
townspeople as would
listen. He called this
innovation the
"whistlestop" campaign.*

linguistics, folklore, and education.

A third member of the Pound family, Olivia, was born in 1874 and also was taught at home, entering the University of Nebraska at age 15. After receiving her degree in education with many honors, including Phi Beta Kappa, she became a member of the staff of the Lincoln public schools, serving as dean of women and assistant principal of Lincoln High School. The sisters lived together in one of Lincoln's spectacular Victorian homes at 1632 L Street.

One of Lincoln's best-known citizens, William Jennings Bryan, was born in 1860 in Salem, Illinois, where his father practiced law and was later made a judge. About the only distinguishing feature of his childhood and university days was that he was orator for his graduating class in both high school and master's law class. He began practicing law in 1883 and on one occasion visited a classmate, A.R. Talbot, in Lincoln. He was so impressed with the city that he determined to move to the prairie capital.

On his arrival in 1887 he established his practice in the Burr Block at 12th and O and, surviving on a scant income, lived for a few months in the office, sleeping on a couch and cooking over a gas ring. It was at this point that he became interested in the Democratic party and began making speeches on its behalf. In 1890 Bryan was elected to the U.S. Congress, where he served two terms. From 1894 to 1896, he was editor of the Omaha *World-Herald*. At the Democratic National Convention in 1896 his keynote address, the still-famous "Cross of Gold" speech, so stirred the delegates that he found himself nominated for the Presidency.

Using his famed powers of oratory, Bryan campaigned more vigorously than virtually any predecessor. It was his idea that by talking directly to the voters, he could convince them of the validity of his candidacy. The result was the nation's first "whistle-stop campaign." He traveled more than 20,000 miles and talked to hundreds of thousands of people, but was defeated nonetheless. He was nominated again in 1900, and that same year he founded his

THE GREAT CAMP MEETINGS OF EPWORTH PARK

In the shadow of the great Methodist camp meeting held at Lake Chautauqua, New York, the Nebraska Epworth League, meeting in Nebraska City in 1892, suggested that an annual assembly be held in Nebraska. Although many cities in Nebraska had held summer camp meetings, the league's proposal called for the creation of a central park with suitable buildings and an auditorium. Four years later the first assembly met in rented tents in Lincoln Park on Salt Creek. (Just to the north, across Calvert Street, lay several hundred acres purchased by the Methodist Epworth League for their future meeting grounds.)

Lincoln Park itself was a first-rate vacation and picnic area, located southwest of First and Van Dorn streets. The park, laid out by H.C. Holt, featured a mile-long horse track and numerous "wild animals" such as buffalo and elk roaming the grounds. Two restaurants and a midway fed and entertained the crowds that numbered as many as 180,000 a year. In 1916 four hundred and fifty incandesent lights and 12 arc lights were added to the park, and it was renamed Electric Park. Featuring open-air dancing and boating, it was known as the "Coney Island of the West." Later, under the ownership of the Burlington Railroad, it was leased to the Boy Scouts who named it Camp Minus Kuya; still later it was purchased by the city of Lincoln for part of the Wilderness Park development.

While the Epworth League continued to meet in Lincoln Park, work was under way to dredge a 200-acre, donut-shaped lake and erect a 3,000-seat amphitheater at a new park. Within a few months Epworth Park was opened for public picnicking and camping. Each summer, however, the area was reserved for a 10-day camp meeting attended by thousands who arrived by rail, wagon, and (later) automobile. Within a few years these 10-day summer meetings became the second largest religious meetings in the United States; only the original Lake Chautauqua meetings were larger in number of attendants.

Season tickets for the "Great Camp Meetin' in the Promised Land" cost one dollar ("no tickets will be sold on Sunday"). Tents rented from two to eight dollars a week, and furniture from 20 cents for a folding chair to 50 cents for a wire cot. Five restaurants were available for those not wishing to cook over kerosene stoves, with "meals of wholesome food served at a cost of 15 to 50 cents—according to your appetite." A first-class grocery and bakery were on the premises, as well as bath houses and other necessities. Railroads provided transportation to Lincoln at half-fare plus 50 cents, and the Lincoln Traction Company ran numerous specials at the gates.

After a few summer sessions proved the popularity and profitability of the camp meetings, a 150-guest frame hotel was built. Rooms were available at 25 cents or 50 cents a night, or they could be reserved for the season. As more and more families began planning their vacations around the camp meetings, the trustees allowed sites to be rented and permanent summer homes constructed. Also, frame and concrete tent cottages could be set up. The result was a virtual village with hundreds of sites on named and numbered streets. Those unable to or not interested in setting aside 10 days would flock to the grounds for evening and weekend concerts. They would come by the hundreds to escape the heat of the city as much as to hear the great speakers, among them William Jennings Bryan, Booker T. Washington, or T. Dewitt Talmadge. Between speakers and WCTU crusades, entertainers—including animal acts, Swiss bell ringers, magicians, and Enrico Caruso—performed. It was not uncommon for the traction company to reserve from 15 to 25 extra cars to carry families back to the city after a particularly big show in the Great Hall, which often had more than 2,000 standing-room-only attendants around the edges.

Each summer one evening was given over to "Venetian Night." Hundreds of canoes and rowboats would be decorated with crepe paper, candles, flowers, and Japanese lanterns, all competing for cash awards of $25, $15, and $10. One barge floated around Oxford Isle, shooting fireworks, while a military band played marches and patriotic music. As memorable as these displays were, Everett Jackman, historian for the Methodist Church, described the lake as one of the finest mosquito-breeding areas and home to one of the most vocal bullfrog colonies in the state.

By the end of World War I, Methodist zeal was waning. The automobile, radio, and movies gave people mobility and new windows on the world previously afforded by Chautauqua and visiting speakers. Attendance dwindled further with the Depression until 1935, when more than a foot of rain fell in a little more than two days and the park was nearly swept off the map. Salt Creek rampaged through the grounds and removed the earthen dam, which consequently flooded the lake. An attempt was made to revive the park, but it was not successful. The remnants of the cabins were moved to either the Blue River near Crete or to Yankee Hill where they were built into homes. Today the entire grounds, like Lincoln Park, are a part of Lincoln's Wilderness Park.

Opposite: This portrait of William Jennings Bryan shows the attorney newly arrived in Lincoln about 1887. During his early, "lean" years there, Bryan often slept in his office (at 12th and O) and occasionally cooked his meals there.

own newspaper, *The Commoner,* in Lincoln. Bryan felt that his home on D Street was not suitable for a potential United States President and began planning "Fairview" at 49th and Sumner, which he envisioned as a "Monticello of the west." He lost in 1900, and again in 1908, but in his campaigns had become well known as an orator and was much sought after on the Chautauqua circuits. He was named Secretary of State by Woodrow Wilson in 1913 and received a great deal of national publicity in 1915 when he resigned in protest over actions that Bryan felt could draw the United States into war with Germany. Bryan died in 1925, a few days after the highly publicized and controversial Scopes

evolution trial, in which he was opposed by Clarence Darrow. At his death Bryan was said to be the highest-priced public speaker in the world, commanding a minimum of $1,000 per appearance. He was said to have spoken directly to more people than any other person in history, a record still standing today because of the modern reliance on radio and television.

Although Bryan was three times a candidate for the Presidency, Charles Dawes of Lincoln actually came closer to the office, being elected Vice-President under Calvin Coolidge in 1924. Dawes arrived in Lincoln at about the same time as Bryan and, like him, began his legal practice in the Burr Block. Real estate became a profitable interest as he began

After teaching at the University of Nebraska and earning an advanced degree there in the 1890s, General John J. Pershing lived in many places but frequently listed Lincoln as his home. He built a house for his sisters in Lincoln, visited them frequently, and left his son in their care upon his wife's death. In this 1921 photograph Pershing poses for sculptor Bryant Baker in Washington, D.C.

acquiring downtown property, including the northwest and southeast corners of 13th and O streets. As a friend of General John J. Pershing, he became United States purchasing agent for the American Expeditionary Force in World War I, with the rank of brigadier general. He had earlier served as comptroller of the currency and in 1921 became the first director of the newly created Bureau of the Budget. The Woods family of Lincoln promoted Dawes as Coolidge's running mate in 1924 when their aggressive efforts on behalf of General Pershing for the office of President failed to bear fruit. In 1925 Dawes won the Nobel Peace Prize for his role in developing the Dawes Plan for German war reparations.

Although he was not born in Lincoln and in fact spent most of his life away from the city, many consider General Pershing another favorite son. Born in Missouri in 1860, Pershing was graduated from the U.S. Military Academy in 1883. In 1891 he attended the University of Nebraska and served as professor of military science and tactics, receiving his LL.B. there in 1923. In addition to this degree Pershing would eventually be awarded honorary doctorates in the United States and Great Britain. When the United States entered World War I in 1917, he became commander of the Allied Expeditionary Force, and in 1919 he was made General of the Armies, a unique rank established by Congress specifically for him. In the same year Mark Woods began a campaign to promote Pershing for President, an offer which he declined to accept. After his wife and three daughters were killed in the burning of the San Francisco Presidio, General Pershing left his son Francis with his two sisters at the home he purchased in Lincoln at 1748 B Street, which he often listed as his own permanent address as well.

Another person often claimed as a Lincolnite actually spent only a few months in the capital city. Charles A. Lindbergh was born in Little Falls, Minnesota, in 1902. After developing an early love for flying, he left for Lincoln on

his motorcycle, arriving on April 1, 1922. There he attended E.J. Sias' Lincoln Flying School at 24th and O. Although he learned to fly in Lincoln with Ira Biffle in a Lincoln Standard airplane, he did not solo until the late summer near Humboldt. Lindbergh gained worldwide prominence in 1927 when he flew from Roosevelt Field, New York, nonstop to Le Bourget, France, becoming the first person to fly the Atlantic nonstop.

On Monday, February 12, 1900, the Lincoln City Auditorium opened on the southeast corner of 13th and M with a concert by Ignace Jan Paderewski, perhaps the most famous and sought-after performer of the decade. Because of his popularity and the desire of the locals to see their new hall, the *Nebraska State Journal* reported that all the one-dollar tickets were soon sold and that it took 40 minutes "to get from the edge of the crowd to within hailing distance of Jake Oppenheimer who was taking tickets at the door." The concert was a great coup for Lincoln and was considered the greatest assemblage of music lovers between Chicago and San Francisco. After the gala opening,

Above: In 1926 Lincoln was one of the leading light aircraft manufacturing centers in the U.S. One of the planes made here was the Lincoln Standard. Pictured is the Lincoln Standard Tourabout in which Charles Lindbergh took lessons in 1921.

Left: Although Charles A. Lindbergh lived in the city less than six months, it was in Lincoln, at the Lincoln Aviation School, that he took his early flight training. Lindbergh is shown with his famous Spirit of St. Louis.

81

a more mundane bill of fare was instituted, and the folding chairs were removed for roller skating when times were slack.

Late at night after the final performance of the university's Kosmet Klub presentation of *The Love Hater* on April 15, 1928, a fire broke out in the props. A previous fire, virtually a year to the day earlier, had already damaged the building, but this one completely destroyed it and caused additional damage to several nearby structures. Although plans to rebuild began the following morning, confusion arose as to who actually owned the building. The American Legion held $11,000 of the $18,000 insurance, with the county, not the city, as beneficiary. While the disagreement thickened, a privately owned auditorium was built on the southeast corner of 10th and M.

The university continued to grow and increase its influence on the legislature as

the 20th century approached. Over the objections of an Omaha faction, which claimed that the state already had too many doctors, a medical college opened in Lincoln in 1883 with 52 students and a budget of $700. Three separate divisions were instituted on what was sometimes referred to as a competing basis: allopathic, eclectic, and homeopathic. Omaha was opposed to a state-sponsored competitor to the Omaha Medical College, arguing that only fifth-raters would apply to Lincoln and that Lincoln had no hospital in which the students could practice. Meanwhile the local populace became nervous over grave-robbing rumors, and a banner reading "cash paid for stiffs" was hung over the front door of University Hall. The chancellor tried to remove the university from the controversy by informing the anatomy professor that he would have to

Above: For a short time, principally before the University of Nebraska had a marching band, the state had its own official group, shown here on the capitol steps in 1909.

Opposite: This group of Lincoln eighth-grade football players posed for a team picture in 1891.

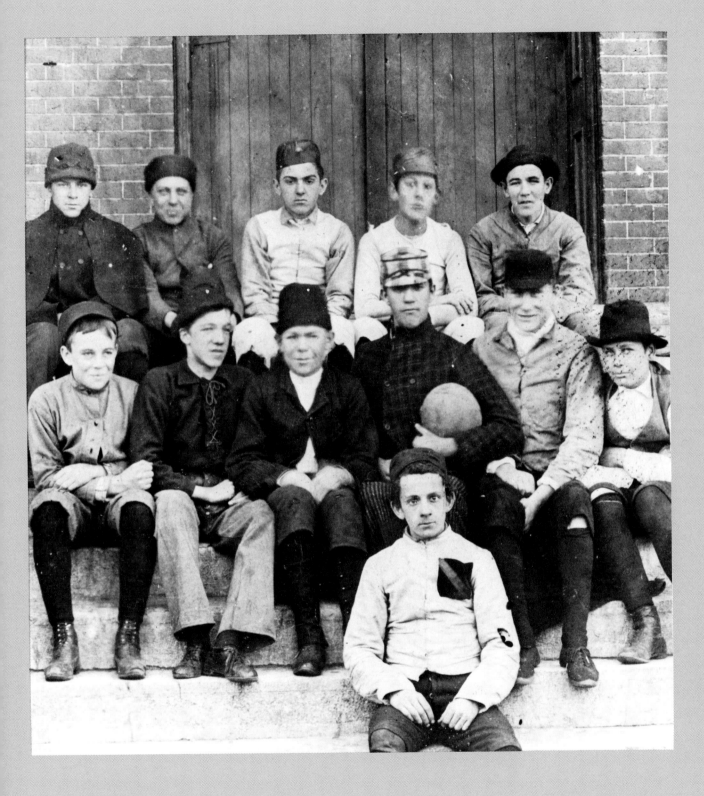

Lincoln postmaster S.M. Melick, seen in his automobile along with several horse-drawn mail wagons, shows off the west loading dock of the new post office as completed in 1906.

personally furnish his own anatomical material. Then a young "working girl" was found murdered in her room above Mollie Hall's Cigar Store, just west of the Lincoln Hotel. The culprit was quickly brought to justice, but not before the victim's body had disappeared from the mortuary. A reporter discovered that the anatomy professor's buggy had been seen in the area, the body suddenly reappeared, and the rumors flew. The publicity forced the regents to close the school of medicine in 1887, and Omaha offered to help in reestablishing the school in their more metropolitan climate.

Academics, however, were not suffering. In 1891 the university absorbed the private Lincoln Central Law College, while in Room 205 in the northeast corner of University Hall, three professors originated a joint seminar in history and economics, the first graduate seminar at the school. From these modest beginnings grew the

first formal graduate school west of the Mississippi.

Baseball, tennis, and track were about to be permanently upstaged when, in 1890, Dr. Langdon Frothingham arrived to teach at the agriculture school and brought a football with him. He became the unofficial and unpaid football coach by popular acclamation—it was his ball. By 1893 the university had its first paid football coach, Frank Crawford. Since then the Nebraska "Bugeaters" have become the Cornhuskers, and the sport has continued to grow in community interest as well as national prominence.

As the student population topped 2,000, several outstate newspapers pointed out that the physical limits of the university had now been reached and proposed moving the campus to the Agriculture Farm or to another city. In 1903 Chancellor E. Benjamin Andrews' classmate, John D. Rockefeller, offered to contribute $66,666.66 toward the construction of a student activities building if the community would match the gift by raising $33,333.33. At first the idea was eagerly embraced by the regents and community, but an editorial in the Omaha *World-Herald* wished a plague on Mr. Rockefeller's "oil-tainted" money and urged people not to contribute to the project, stating that soon Rockefeller would try to control the faculty and regents. William Jennings Bryan sided with the opponents and was parodied in the student paper, the *Daily Nebraskan.*

Praise John from whom "oil" blessings flow,
Praise also Bill who spends the dough;
Praise John, Praise Bill, Praise all the host;
Praise Bill a little; praise John the most.

In 1906 ground was broken for the building, known as the Temple, after an ingenious way had been found to accept the "ill-earned" gift. The building was erected outside the defined campus on the southeast corner of 12th and R, and title was given to the "students of the University of Nebraska."

By the turn of the century the population of the city had reached 40,000, and the federal government began investigating the erection of a new U.S. post office and federal courthouse on the northern half of the post office block. In 1902 the government decided to go ahead with the proposal, and negotiations began to transfer the old post office to the city for the sum of $50,000 for use as a city hall, with title to be vested in the city so long as the building was used for municipal purposes. The city, which had moved from various rented quarters to rooms above the fire and police departments on New Haymarket Square, was eager to have a permanent, albeit over-spacious, headquarters. In 1906 the post office moved into its new $350,000 Second Renaissance Revival-style building at 10th and P streets. The city took possession of the old building and began remodeling it. At this time the saltwater fountain was in a corner created by the

Top: Built in 1870, old University Hall was the first building on the University of Nebraska campus. In 1924 the building was declared unsafe for further use, and the tower and upper floors were removed. The first floor and basement were roofed over and continued in use until the building was razed in 1949. Courtesy, University of Nebraska-Lincoln Archives

Above: When the new science building was completed north of the Lincoln High School in 1885, its facilities, seen in this photo, were considered among the finest west of the Missouri River.

Above: The 45th, Fifth, and later the Sixth regiments of the Nebraska National Guard were ordered to New Mexico in 1915, ostensibly to protect the country's Mexican border. This was later shown to be part of Wilson's plan to prepare for possible war when the guard was moved to Germany. The young man pictured shyly bids goodbye at Lincoln's Burlington Station, as Company A of the Fifth Nebraska Regiment prepares to leave. From the author's collection

Opposite: By July 22, 1918, when this photo was taken in the middle of 13th and O streets looking north, Lincoln had joined the rest of the nation in patriotic zeal. These men hold up signs that not-too-subtly encourage enlistment.

Above right: After armistice, Lincoln celebrated the return of its sons. This man's sign summed up the city's and the country's feelings.

two structures. In 1915 the post office created a $250,000 addition, and the resulting building occupied about two-thirds of the northern half of the block, thus hiding the fountain on three sides. The fountain was then moved west from the center of the block, nearly to 9th Street, and a pump was added to move the salt water from the well.

In 1909 the city of Lincoln voted "dry" after having had liquor by the drink for nearly 40 years. The liquor lobby sought to negate this economic turn of events and, in league with a removalist group, began investigating the calling of an election to remove the capital from Lincoln. By suggesting a change in the legislative language, they thought they could easily gain the support of several contenders, including Grand Island and Kearney. Two bills were introduced, but both ultimately failed. According to State Historical Society director A.E. Sheldon, "The people of Lincoln were so badly scared that at the election in May following the adjournment of the legislature, the saloons were voted in again."

The original high school, which had been extravagantly large when completed, was added onto in 1895 and 1902. By 1905 it was considered overcrowded, and talk of a new building began. In 1909 the school board, now committed to the erection of a new building, advanced several proposals. The first, and least desirable in their eyes, was to build on the old 15th and M property. The other sites included 14th and A, 22nd and J, and 17th and K. At first the possibility of two schools, one south and one east of the city, existed, but ultimately the two favorites came down to the existing site and the Davenport Tract at 22nd and J. Proponents of the old site pointed out that the city already owned the land and that it was centrally located, whereas the Davenport Tract was adjacent to the railroad, there was no bridge over Antelope Creek, the site was in the flood plain, and the location was undesirable because of its continued use as a tent-show and circus site. The other faction pointed

out that if the old site were reemployed, there would be no place to hold classes during construction, there were saloons and other evil establishments too close for comfort downtown, the residential population was rapidly growing to the south and east, and the actual building site at 22nd and J was not only pleasant but well above the flood plain of Antelope Creek. The solution was to send ballots home with the students. Amid flaring tempers, newspaper editorials, and numerous speaking and handbill canvasses on both sides, the parents chose the 22nd and J site. In 1911 bonds were approved, in 1912 the property was secured, in 1913 the cornerstone was laid, and in September 1915 the $750,000 building was occupied. The old structure was used as an administration complex until 1941, when the board of education purchased the Bonacum Institute building just south of Lincoln High School for its administrative offices. The Bonacum (Catholic) High School had been started in 1931, but the financing fell through during the Depression, leaving the building empty and uncompleted.

When World War I broke out in 1914, a substantial minority of Lincoln's population was of German extraction. A century and a half earlier, in 1764, large colonies of emigrants from Germany had responded to an invitation from Russian Czarina Catherine the Great to settle in Russia, primarily along the Volga River. They were promised free land, freedom of religion, no taxation for up to 30 years, interest-free loans, and exemption from military conscription. The plan was readily accepted, and by 1915 the population of the German communities in Russia reached nearly three quarters of a million. By 1870, however, many of the promises had run out or were being ignored by the Russian government, and an exodus of sorts began. Lincoln and the Great Plains attracted many of these German-Russians because of the climate, agrarian communities, and a general feeling of welcome. By the time the inflow stopped in 1914, more than one-third of Lincoln's population was made up

of these German-Russian immigrants and their descendants.

In 1915 William Jennings Bryan resigned from his position as Secretary of State in protest against actions of President Woodrow Wilson that Bryan felt could lead the nation into war with Germany. Senator George Norris of Nebraska also argued against Wilson and on April 6, 1917, voted against the declaration of war. Nonetheless, the nation and Lincoln were at war. The Nebraska National Guard, which had been sent to the Mexican border with General Pershing in 1916, was recalled in 1917. The declaration of war unified the county, and nearly 4,000 men enlisted. The nearby communities of Berlin and Germantown changed their names to Otoe and Garland; the study of German was entirely eliminated from school curriculums; shopkeepers forbade employees to speak German with customers; the German-American Bank became the Continental State Bank; and members of Lincoln's German community found themselves scrutinized at every turn. In addition, with the surge of patriotism, eight University of Nebraska faculty members were charged with a "lack of aggressive loyalty," culminating in the dismissal of three.

University Chancellor Samuel Avery offered the army use of the facilities of the school's mechanical engineering department, and in June 1918, nine hundred men arrived for training. Barracks were constructed on the farm campus, while other men were quartered in the uncompleted Social Sciences Building and fed in the basement of the Temple.

On November 11, 1918, the armistice was signed, and the city celebrated. Of the 3,990 Lancaster County volunteers, 90 had been killed in action. While the war had interrupted Lincoln's growth, the end of armed hostilities found the city eager to pick up shelved plans and begin new ones, revolving around a large number of returning men eager for university education, the fund drive for and construction of Memorial Stadium, and planning for a new statehouse.

Above: This architect's rendering of the state capitol building was done by the architectural firm of Bertram Grosvenor Goodhue. Goodhue designed the building, which is listed as one of the architectural wonders of the world. The unsigned painting is the architect's conception of the building. However, the capitol was completed after Goodhue's death, and a number of changes were incorporated into the finished structure.

The Nebraska State Capitol towers 400 feet above the city of Lincoln. During the past decade the city has planted hundreds of flowering trees throughout the downtown. Flowering crab set off the Sower and the capitol each spring in spectacular color. Aerial view courtesy, Nebraska Game and Parks Commission. Photo at left by Randy Hampton, Journal-Star Printing Company

One of the most attractive areas at the Nebraska State Fair is sponsored by the Nebraska Game and Parks Commission. The exhibit includes wildlife habitats, a live show, and many interesting displays. Photo by Randy Hampton, Journal-Star Printing Company

Above: Wilderness Park covers nearly 1,500 acres and encompasses some old Lincoln parks, native stands of timber, and unbroken prairie grass. More than 17 miles of riding and hiking trails provide a great escape from the nearby city. Courtesy, Nebraska Game and Parks Commission

Left: Spring flowers line the central courtyard of Gateway Shopping Center, 61st and O streets. Photo by Randy Hampton, Journal-Star Printing Company

93

A hot-air balloon passes over a farm south of Lincoln near Highway Two. Photo by Bruce E. Wendorff

Right: Lincoln youths are shown competing in a bicycle race at the northeast branch of the YMCA. The races are held every Saturday morning during the summer months. Photo by Bruce E. Wendorff

Above: As fall arrives, the city's trees cover the streets, yards, and cars with a colorful blanket of leaves. Photo by Steve Traudt

Left: Pioneers Park is seen on a clear day in winter. Courtesy, Nebraska Game and Parks Commission

Below: As part of the Antelope Creek Watershed, the U.S. Army Corps of Engineers flooded over 500 acres of farmland, forming Holmes Park Lake. The lake is a favorite sailing and sunning area during the summer and provides the background for the city-sponsored annual Fourth of July fireworks show. Photo by Joel Sartore

Lincoln's Pioneers Park provides an excellent spot for this family to walk, picnic, or take one of the nature hikes in the park's Chet Ager Nature Center. Photo by Randy Hampton, Journal-Star Printing Company

A member of the University of Nebraska marching band waits to begin his half-time performance with the Memorial Stadium crowd reflected in his horn. Photo by Steve Traudt

Above: Autumn Saturday afternoons find Lincoln's Memorial Stadium packed to the hilt as the University of Nebraska Cornhuskers battle for victory. Thousands of red balloons are released by cheering fans after Nebraska's first score at each home game. Courtesy, Nebraska Game and Parks Commission

Right: A crowd is on hand as University of Nebraska students compete in a game of "Oozeball," or mud volleyball. Photo by Steve Traudt

Above: The Nebraska State Fair is held in Lincoln each year on grounds located just northeast of the University of Nebraska campus. Here workers are shown readying a display for the 1983 edition of the fair in front of one of the new structures. Photo by Randy Hampton, Journal-Star Printing Company

Left: Both the university curriculum and the Nebraska State Fair remind Lincolnites of the importance of agriculture to the region. University of Nebraska employee Phil Anderson collects eggs at the East Campus experimental agricultural farm. Photo by John Goecke

Opposite: Thousands of Nebraskans travel to the annual state fair. Most of those who make the annual trek end up on the midway and its popular rides. Photo by Steve Traudt

The annual Native Americans Week is sponsored by the University of Nebraska-Lincoln Campus Activities and Programming Native American Special Events Committee and the Nebraska American Student Congress. Photo by Bruce E. Wendorff

Above: A Lincoln family takes advantage of a warm day to picnic in Pioneers Park. The park's bronze buffalo statue, cast in Paris by G. Gaudet, stands in the background. Photo by Randy Hampton, Journal-Star Printing Company

Right: Accompanied only by his shadow, a runner makes his way through the Lincoln Marathon. Photo by Steve Traudt

CHAPTER **VI**

LINCOLN IN THE 20TH CENTURY

This night view from the Nebraska State Capitol looks northwest over Lincoln's downtown. Photo by Steve Traudt

By 1901 the second state capitol had begun to settle. Remembering the early demise of the first, poorly constructed building, the citizenry and legislature were a bit uneasy. One report had it that an early well or sandpit at the southeast corner of the building could be collapsing, causing settling in that area. By 1908 the corner had sunk six to eight inches, resulting in falling plaster, doors that would no longer close, and shattered windowpanes. As the problems continued, coupled with crumbling stonework and inadequate office space, talk of a new structure, perhaps as a memorial to World War I veterans, began in earnest. In 1917 repairs were begun, but the extent of required repairs proved, even to the most skeptical, that a new building was the only real solution.

On February 20, 1919, the 37th session of the legislature passed HR 3, which provided for an unpaid commission to establish a contest for plans for a new capitol, not to cost more than five million dollars, and to oversee the construction. The bill also covered financing, which was to be accomplished by a $1.5-million levy against the grand assessment of the state. The members of the commission were Governor Sam McKelvie; George E. Johnson, the state engineer; Walter W. Head; William Thompson; and William Hardy. They chose Omaha architect Thomas R. Kimball, president of the American Institute of Architects, as counsel and drew up the rules of the competition.

The commission's design guidelines stated that the new building should "be a

practical, working home for the government; that it be an inspiring, beautiful monument worthy of the state; and that it be accomplished without scandal, friction, extravagance, or waste in order to inspire pride in every Nebraskan." The commission sought a symbol of and for the state, not just a statehouse. The first stage of the competition was limited to Nebraska architects. Three designs were to be chosen; each would receive a prize of $500 and would be entered in the final competition. The Nebraska firms chosen were Ellery Davis of Lincoln, John Latenser and Sons of Omaha, and John and Alan McDonald of Omaha. In the next phase invitations were sent to a number of nationally prominent architects. In order to preserve anonymity, all designs were numbered. The judges' final deliberations began in June 1920.

All the designs rested heavily on the classic federal domed capitol design, except those of Ellery Davis and Bertram Grosvenor Goodhue, which featured towers. Davis' tower and building design followed the Beaux Arts school. After three days of discussion, the plan with the greatest departure from the dominant theme was chosen, Goodhue's tower. Second place went to John R. Pope of New York and third place to McKim, Mead, and White of New York. The distinctive design was certainly a strong point, but Goodhue's four-acre, 400-foot high building was also the most cost-size effective and allowed for possible expansion. Pragmatically, Goodhue was also the only contestant who foresaw the costly

Above: In 1920 the Daughters of the Founders and Patriots of America was founded in Lincoln. This photo shows a group of the charter members.

Top: The longest straight main street in the world, Lincoln's O Street, is shown in the 1930s, looking east from 11th Street.

necessity of relocating the capitol tenants during construction and devised a building that could be built on a pay-as-you-go basis while the former structure was occupied and not razed until after the new structure became usable. The radical design was not without its detractors, but surprisingly, the conservative Nebraska populace was nearly unanimous in its support of the unique capitol design.

The first physical evidences that construction was about to begin were the felling of numerous trees on the grounds in the spring of 1922 and the laying of the first tracks for the Capitol Commission Railroad. This nearly mile-long connection via H Street from the capitol grounds to the Burlington main track at 7th Street was a source of some concern. It had been determined that trucking the building materials in would destroy the residential paving, but local citizens were more concerned about the noise and smoke from a railroad running past their homes. The problem was solved when the H Street Railway was fitted with a quiet, diesel-electric engine, giving Nebraska the honor of having the only state-owned railway in the nation. Though less than a mile long, including a quarter-mile track on the four-block construction site, the "Haitch Street" system ultimately saved the state more than $100,000 in hauling fees.

THE STATE CAPITOL:
AN ILLUSTRATION OF NEBRASKA HISTORY

It is impossible to separate symbolism and the capitol building: they are connected in every conceivable way. Each element, whether designed by Bertram Grosvenor Goodhue, implemented by the sculpture of Lee Lawrie, the art of Hildreth Meière, August Vincent Tack, and Elizabeth Dolan, or the inscriptions of Hartley Burr Alexander, contributes to the total. The art that is found throughout the building is part of the overall theme Goodhue called "that combination of action and thought which is the essence of all human life, social as well as individual."

The general symbolism of the complete structure begins with the lower stories, clinging to the earth, furnishing a "dramatic platform upon which uprears, like the circumvallation of an olden town, the low horizontal square of the outer edifice. Within this wall-like structure the transepts shape the four court while at the crux, the central tower sweeps sheerly upward. It is geometrically simple. And its horizontal and vertical movements are readily symbolically translated as the level progress of history and the rising attitudes of the ideal." At the base of the tower are eight figures: Penaour, an Egyptian scribe and poet representing history; Ezekiel, a prophet of Israel, for vision; Socrates, a Greek philosopher, for reason; Marcus Aurelius, for the state; the apostle John, for faith; Louis IX, for chivalry; Newton, for science; and Abraham Lincoln, for liberty.

The main north entrance and facade serve as a preface to the building and its symbols. They illustrate the history of Nebraska through the use of Indian motifs and inscriptions translated from ceremonial songs, and with the pioneers' Great Plains settlement. The east and west balustrades to the sides of the capitol steps read "honor to citizens who build an house of state where men live well" and "honor to pioneers who broke the sods that men to come might live."

Dr. Alexander originally wrote "honor," but Goodhue unconsciously substituted "honour." Later he telegraphed: "Am disturbed about omission of U in 'honour' in inscriptions. Prefer U on both artistic and philological grounds, especially since fourth line at right reads 'an house.' Please wire decision." Alexander himself immediately agreed but later noted that one of the first criticisms was the Anglicization "of *American* spellings—and with a 'v' for a 'u' in Honovr!"

Above the north door and below a frieze of corn and buffalo, is a bas-relief with a two-tone gold background by Lee Lawrie titled *The Spirit of the Pioneers*. The inscription above the door declares, "The salvation of the state is watchfulness in the citizen." On each side of the building is a stone carving containing part of the story of the development of the law. Two pairs of figures stand atop the pylon on either side of the main entrance: Wisdom and Justice on the left, with the seal of the United States; and on the right, Power and Mercy, with the Nebraska state seal.

Eighteen spectacular bas-relief panels on the four sides of the building depict great moments in the establishment and execution of laws, from Moses delivering the law as he received it on Mount Sinai, to the Mayflower Compact, the Emancipation Proclamation, the Louisiana Purchase, and the admission of Nebraska as a state. Carved above the windows around the base of the building are the names of each of the 93 counties in Nebraska. *The Sower,* seen. . .is said to "sow the seeds of good government for present and future generations." The capitol's dome represents the sun and sits atop mosaics of the Thunderbird of Indian folklore.

The basic theme of the interior also begins at the north entrance. Here the artwork, more colorful than the exterior, depicts the efforts of Nebraskans to obtain a noble and refined way of life. This theme begins in the vestibule and continues through the foyer or Great Hall to the Rotunda, which contains the entrances to the legislative chambers. It is seen in the mosaic floor tiles, murals, stone carvings, chandeliers, bronze light fixtures, dome art, busts, and wall panels. In the foyer the windows are set in marble frames; and onyx is used in place of glass to soften the sunlight. Balustrades are carved in Utah onyx and contain objects such as buffalo skulls, corn, and birds.

In Memorial Hall atop the tower are inscriptions indicating the room's dedication to heroism called for in public service and in devotion to humanity. Charles Harris Whitaker describes the Nebraska State Capitol as: "the gossamer web of dreams. . .its enduring essence is proportion. Its glory is simplicity."

Above: The "tower on the plains" is shown nearing completion in this 1929 aerial view, looking southeast.

Top: Nebraska Governor Samuel McKelvie breaks the ground for the new state capitol building in Lincoln on April 15, 1922.

Opposite: This interesting photo shows the new capitol being built around the old one, about 1923. This view is looking to the southeast and shows the old heating plant smokestack at right. Note also the wide gap in the west portion of the new building where the old building will be removed and the senate chamber will ultimately be built.

On April 15, 1922, French Field Marshal Joffre, known internationally as the "hero of the Marne," joined Governor McKelvie in breaking ground for the new capitol with a plow pulled by two white horses. With the trees and sidewalks removed and the railroad in place, the Assenmacher Construction Company began digging for the basement and footings in the late spring. As dirt was removed from the excavation site, it was transferred to railroad cars which carried it to the fairgrounds for use as landfill. On Armistice Day, November 11, 1922, the three-ton cornerstone was laid by Alvin Owsley, national commander-in-chief of the American Legion, as Governor McKelvie reset the old building's cornerstone adjacent to it.

Phase one of the construction continued around the old building with only minor inconvenience to statehouse employees and legislators, who had an entry corridor through the west edge of the quadrangle. In late 1924 and early 1925 the outside sections were completed and occupied. It had long since become apparent that the original estimate of five million dollars was far too low, and in March 1925 new legislation provided that the cost of the building must not exceed nine million dollars. By late summer the $43,665 contract for removing the old capitol had been completed, requiring only 70 days. Work on the tower began in September 1925.

Goodhue chose sculptor Lee Lawrie to design and execute the stone carvings and sculpture as well as the *Sower*, which symbolized Nebraska's chief industry, agriculture. The bronze giant was shipped from the New York foundry in an open car and, on arrival in Lincoln, was found to have the word "BOZO" scrawled in chalk across his chest. In order to avoid further vandalism, it was decided to hoist the statue to the 15th floor, there to be stored until the dome and steel superstructure were ready for his final placement. On Thursday, April 24, 1930, a crowd gathered on the site to witness the 7.5-ton, 19-foot *Sower's* ascension. After a protective coating of beeswax was applied,

the *Sower* began his 15-minute, 400-foot ride. As soon as the 12-foot bronze pedestal was ready, the *Sower* was bolted in place, ready to serve as a spectacular cap to the building, visible for more than 20 miles, and to provide an almost perfect lightning rod.

As the tower was ready for use, the west front was enclosed, and construction was completed. In 1934 Nebraska voted to dissolve its two-house legislature in favor of a unicameral state government. This required enlarging the west chamber, omitting the planned domed ceiling. Grading and landscaping were completed in 1933, though not to Goodhue's specifications, and the final cost was calculated at just over $9.8 million.

Although observers claim completion dates for the capitol ranging from 1932 to 1964, the building remains formally undedicated. In 1955 an editorial pointed out the glaring omission, but no action was taken. In 1964 Senator Hugo Srb suggested that the centennial year of 1976 would be an excellent opportunity for the dedication. Others felt that when the building was placed on the national registry of historic buildings in October 1976, a dedication would be fitting. Finally it was decided to stage the official dedication during the construction semicentennial in 1982. The fact remains, however, that the building has still never received its final dedication, and because Goodhue purposely left areas to be completed by future generations—such areas as the courtyards are currently moving toward completion—it may never truly be completed or dedicated.

Before the building was even ready for use, artists, engineers, and architects worldwide realized that the capitol represented far more than anticipated; indeed, in a poll of 500 architects it was voted one of the 10 most beautiful buildings in the world and fourth among the 25 best-built structures of all time. Honors grew daily; one group, the Palos Verdes Art Jury, considering all buildings ever built in the United States from the first colonial settlements, rated the capitol as the number-one example of artistic and creative achievement. Not the least of the plaudits, according to many Nebraskans, was that Nebraska's was the only state capitol ever to be completely paid for at the time of its completion.

For all its beauty and vast detail, the capitol was virtually finished in just over 10 years, though even now some of the original plans and landscaping are being completed. For detailed descriptions of the thousands of carvings, mosaics, art works, and inscriptions, the reader should consult the October 1934 issue of *American Architect* and *The Architectural Wonder of the World* (1965) by Elinor L. Brown.

Although the building of the capitol appeared to progress peacefully and methodically, the architect and the commissioners overseeing the building, particularly state engineer George E. Johnson, were frequently at odds, beginning with Goodhue's determination that the building should face north. State engineer Johnson claimed a west front would be more appropriate, because it would allow the building to capture the afternoon sun. Johnson was sure that Goodhue was bilking the state on expensive ideas and materials and at one point demanded that even the art work and stone sculpture be put out for bids. The arguments culminated in Johnson's demanding that Goodhue be fired and replaced. In apology, the *House Journal* of 1923 publicly lauded Goodhue and called for the expunging of all criticisms from the record. Even this did not satisfy or silence Johnson, who continued to question many decisions as well as the salary Goodhue received to oversee construction. On April 23, 1924, Bertram G. Goodhue died suddenly at his home in Connecticut. His wife and a number of colleagues agreed that the harassment and political insults he had suffered in Nebraska contributed to his early death at the age of 55. His firm was chosen to continue the project, however, and today the capitol stands as an enduring monument to the man himself as well as to the people of the state.

Another enduring monument to the

THE STUART THEATER: FROM CREATION TO RENOVATION

In 1927 Charles Stuart, Sr., commissioned Ellery L. Davis, Sr., and W.F. Wilson of Lincoln to prepare plans for a major office/ theater building to be built on the southeast corner of 13th and P streets. On the one-time site of the Lyric Theater and Nebraska Buick Auto Company, a $1.25 million, 13-story structure was designed and built for Stuart in one year. Primarily Gothic in its construction, the building was faced with Bedford and Indiana limestone, and its interior details were set in marble, bronze, and wrought iron.

The first tenants moved into their offices in 1928, but the grand opening did not occur until 1929 when the theater was completed. The theater occupied about half of each of the first six floors, with the other half and all of the next four floors devoted to office space. The top three floors, which had a dining room and sports court facilities, were leased to a private club.

On Monday, June 10, 1929, the Stuart Theater opened with a seven-part, four-hour program featuring the western premier of a "talking" film, *The Rainbow Man,* a "talking" Our Gang film, Vitaphone and Movietone News, Don Pedro and the Stuart Stage Band, and a topical short entitled *The Spice of Life.* Also included were speeches by Governor Arthur J. Weaver and Mayor Don L. Love, plus introductions of numerous persons involved in the building's construction and management. The first ticket, sold to Eli Shire, manager of the Lincoln Theater Company, was cast in solid gold and given to the State Historical Society's archives. And the opening-night, one-dollar price gave way to evening prices of 60 cents and matinee prices of 40 cents.

The theater itself was called the "second best building in the state," and not as over-dramatic as some of the West Coast theaters. The architecture was described as Italian Romanesque, Moorish, Gallic, and Spanish. Its ceilings were beamed and paneled with round panels designed after Roman chariot wheels. The auditorium walls resembled the exterior of old Italian palaces. Six chandeliers hung in pairs; the two largest weighed 2.5 tons each, were 16 feet tall, used 450 electric bulbs each, and could be lowered by cables for cleaning and maintenance.

Also in the auditorium, which seated 1,856 and was air-conditioned, was one of the largest totally appliqued and embroidered velvet stage curtains ever produced. The curtain itself was Italian red with antique green and gold lattice, and had peacock blue fleur-de-lis panels.

In 1972, as Omaha spent just over $2 million to restore its Orpheum Theater, the Stuart Theater was leased to the Dubinsky Brothers Theaters. What was announced as a remodeling proved to be nearly total destruction of the original theater and its decor. The stage, once used by vaudeville, the Lincoln Symphony Orchestra, and touring play groups, was walled off to create a bar. The chandeliers were removed and a false ceiling installed. The terra cotta side balconies and decorations were air-hammered, chiseled away, and hidden with curtains. The orchestra pit was covered with plywood and the spectacular proscenium draped. On the lower-level the lounges and balconies were sealed off, and much of the wood and original stenciling was painted over.

In 1977, when the James Stuart family announced that the theater and first five floors of the Stuart Building had been given to the University of Nebraska Foundation, preservationists and a "Save the Stuart" committee thought a restoration project could be proposed. Studying the possibility of renovating the theater and enlarging the stage, a task force turned in mixed reports, which generally suggested that potential seating capacity would not be great enough to support the project. Today, adumbrated and sterile, the Stuart Theater is firmly in business. And more than a decade of Lincoln moviegoers are unaware that one need only climb up to the new projection booth and look out over the top of the suspended ceiling to see the upper portion and balconies of a once-spectacular Stuart Theater.

A crowd gathered outside the Stuart Theater in November 1983 for the Lincoln benefit premiere of Terms of Endearment. Courtesy, Journal-Star Printing Company

The Harley Drug Company was located at 11th and O streets. The adjacent photo was taken inside during a one-cent sale that was so successful a policeman was on hand to maintain order.

foresight of one prominent Lincolnite is Pioneers Park, originally created by John F. Harris in honor of his parents.

When George Harris came to Lincoln in 1871 as a land agent for the Burlington and Missouri River Railroad, the city had only one real park, Lincoln Park at 8th and D streets. Harris' children prospered. Sarah B. Harris became editor of the Lincoln *Courier,* George B. Harris president of the Burlington, and John F. Harris a member of a prominent New York stock brokerage. In 1928 John called his old classmate George Woods and asked him to secure a tract of land in or near Lincoln that could be developed as a memorial to his parents. Woods secured a 500-acre tract southwest of the city and, with the help of Park Superintendent Chet Ager and architect

Ernst Herminghaus, drafted a proposed layout. Harris was so impressed with the plan that he purchased an additional 100 acres and decided to name the area Pioneers Park to honor all pioneers, rather than just his parents. As the park took shape and thousands of trees were planted, many Lincolnites scoffed at the location as being so far away from the city that it would never see popular use. A formal dedication was set for June 2, 1929, featuring Paul Whiteman and his band. Unfortunately, a solid week of rain made the park a sea of mud, and although Whiteman gave an impromptu concert at the railroad station, the festivities were "postponed till July or indefinitely." Finally, on May 17, 1930, the temporary golf course and park were officially, though less formally, dedicated.

Harris also commissioned the bronze casting of a buffalo, located in the circle at the park's entrance. Designed and sculpted in Paris by George Gaudet, the statue was tossed madly about during its ocean voyage, lost by the railroad, narrowly avoided a collision, and finally almost collapsed the wooden bridge across a local creek. Later, as part of the Federal Emergency Relief Program during the Depression, the city, by paying $50 for materials, was able to secure Ellis Burman's 14-foot, five-ton *Smoke Signal* statue for one of the park's knolls. At the dedication, in September 1935, a group of chiefs and members of the Omaha, Winnebago, Sioux, and Ponca Indian tribes camped on the site. Throughout the ceremony many of the Indians sat on their horses at the top of a hill, facing west toward the setting sun. In 1946 Pinewood Bowl was created in the natural amphitheater just north of the *Smoke Signal*, and in September 1964 the Chet Ager Bird and Wildlife Nature Study Center was formed from 40 acres of pond, swamp, and native prairie on the western edge of the park, just east of the outdoor zoo.

The morning of September 17, 1930, began like any other warm fall day in Lincoln, but by noon the capital city could claim the dubious honor of being the bank robbery center of the nation, resplendent with gangland desperadoes and a wild chase.

In 1930 the northwest corner of 12th and O held the Ganter Block, home of the Lincoln National Bank. At 10:02 a.m. four men carrying pillowcases or blankets entered the bank, ordered the employees to lie face down on the floor, and asked for Harold Lionberger, who had the keys to the vault. Ironically, the vault was already open, and in a few minutes the four methodically removed $2,702,796 in cash and securities. Meanwhile, Homer "Big George" Wilson waited with one foot on the running board of their black Buick sedan and casually cradled a Thompson submachine gun, while a "runner" stood by to carry messages back and forth from the bank. After only a few minutes Big George

was approached by two policemen—naturally curious about the machine gun—who were calmly told to scram. The policemen obediently left for the police station in their radioless car. Big George dispatched the runner, telling the men inside to finish up quickly. A minute later, at 10:10, the gang peacefully climbed into their Buick and left, having pulled the world's largest cash bank robbery.

One popular but unsubstantiated rumor of the day claimed that the Buick then doubled back to P Street and drove into a large van, which again drove past the bank and west out of town. Another held that the same Buick had a flat tire south of Omaha and that a farmer who happened by to render aid was convinced that the arsenal of machine guns, rifles, and shotguns was being used to hunt ducks. The most probable scenario is that they simply headed directly south, stayed in Kansas that evening, and spent the next night with H.A. Cunningham of Milan, Missouri, before disappearing into the Ozarks.

The 1918 edition of the Lincoln City Directory lists John Wallace as a sculptor, residing at 1618 O Street. This work of his, made of Washington-brand lard, was displayed in a local merchant's window. An accompanying sign stated, "Is as good as it looks."

The details of the case, as they ultimately came out in court, were more factual but hardly less colorful. Dewey Berlovich, caught attempting to sell $10,900 worth of Liberty bonds to New York attorney F.P. Ferguson, who allegedly had already disposed of $50,000 worth to Eastern banks at 82 to 85 cents on the dollar, was subpoenaed to appear before a federal grand jury. Although Lancaster County Attorney Max Towle thought Berlovich innocent of participation in the actual robbery, he held Berlovich in an attempt to learn the names of those who were involved. Robert Van Pelt, then Assistant United States District Attorney, was asked by state officials to help in the case; even though the bank involved was federally chartered, the robbery was a state and not a federal offense, unless it proved to be an inside job. Van Pelt called upon Leonard Keeler of Northwestern University and his newly perfected "lie detector," which would have marked the machine's first use in Nebraska. Berlovich, however, was so frightened by the machine that he promptly volunteered several names to authorities rather than be subjected to its use.

Meanwhile Gus Winkler, of the famed Al Capone gang, was overheard mumbling about the robbery when police hospitalized him after an auto accident in Chicago. An anonymous group of prominent Chicago businessmen known only as the "Secret Six" sent an attorney to Lincoln to help with the case, believing that there were Capone gang connections. The investigation moved slowly until eyewitnesses identified Tommy "Pat" O'Connor of East St. Louis, Illinois. After staking out O'Connor's East St. Louis apartment for nearly a week, police raided it and arrested six suspects. Besides O'Connor, those taken into custody were Edward O'Hara, Jack Britt, Howard "Pop" Lee, William McQuillen, and Tommy Hayes. Of the six apprehended, Tommy O'Connor, Jack Britt, and Howard Lee were tried in September 1931. Lee was released when two trials ended in hung juries. Although 17 eyewitnesses swore that all six never left Illinois on the day of the robbery, the others were found guilty and served about 10 years each. While the trials were in progress, the Secret Six, working with Gus Winkler, arranged for Lancaster County Attorney Max Towle to go to a Chicago hotel room at 2 a.m. to pick up a suitcase containing $583,000 in Liberty bonds and securities, along with a statement that two million dollars had been burned. Winkler, afraid that his alibi might not hold up in court, in effect traded the bonds for immunity from prosecution.

The Lincoln National Bank closed its doors for good, but the salvaged bonds saved at least five Lancaster County banks, and by diligently working for nearly 15 years at $50 a month, the bank's president, W.A. Selleck, with the backing of the Continental National Bank, paid back the depositors and stockholders in full. Gus Winkler and Dewey Berlovich were both killed within a year.

Through the years, as more information became available, it was suggested by those involved in both the prosecution and defense of the trials that both Lee and O'Connor were innocent and that the guilty probably included George "Machine Gun" Kelly (then referred to as "Big George" Wilson), Willie Vance, Charlie (or Eddy) Fitzgerald, Eddie Dahl (or Larue), Avery Simmons, and possibly Jim Wilson and others. Subsequent to the trials it was also learned that a few months before the robbery a salesman had surveyed the vaults to make recommendations on how to improve security conditions, but more probably to determine how much was kept in the vault and exactly where it was. Many facts are still unclear—but for cash bank robberies, Lincoln still holds the record.

At about the same time Lincoln's banks were being robbed, the effects of the Depression were beginning to settle into the capital city. For most of Nebraska, the Depression began years before the Wall Street collapse in October 1929, and yet Lincoln was able to maintain itself up until 1931. Even then, Lincoln was in a better situation than the rest of the state.

Although farming was the predominant

industry throughout Nebraska—and hit hard in the pre-Depression/Depression years—Lincoln's economy kept afloat. There were construction jobs: the state capitol, the Stuart building, the Sharp building, and several smaller projects were all underway. In addition, the population of Lincoln was growing, partially as a move from the farms, which fed retail sales for a time. The residents of Lincoln, like their rural neighbors, were not heavy investors in the stock market; however, the bank closings disrupted all business and depositors in the area.

In 1932 the Lincoln Trust Company filed for bankruptcy, taking two million dollars in deposits and stockholdings with it. In 1932 as well, the Lincoln *Star* and Lincoln *Journal* merged many of their operations, resulting in one printing plant, one advertising division, and two editorial staffs. Many firms and public employees agreed to pay cuts rather than risk reduction of labor forces; the university employees all took a 10 percent reduction in salaries; and the fire department agreed to work free days. Along with the empty downtown storefronts, the Depression reduced bank deposits by one-third between October 1929 and 1933.

As if the earlier farm depression and the Wall Street collapse were not enough, the mid-'30s produced a drought of an unparalled nature. Off and on for more than three years topsoil drifted like snow in Lincoln, smothering livestock and crops, blocking out the noonday sun, and obscuring the upper floors of the capitol. It was not uncommon during that time for Lincoln to have its streetlights lit in the early afternoon and to see children on their way to school with moistened handkerchiefs over their faces to keep the dust out.

Lincoln's economy was somewhat stabilized by government offices, including the Works Progress Administration (WPA), and Agricultural Adjustment Adminis-tration, as well as its universities; although Cotner College did close its doors permanently as a result of the Depression.

As governmental aid and works projects

came into being, Lincoln wholesale fruit and grocery merchant Harry Grainger conceived a food-stamp plan for the distribution of food to needy individuals and families. Grainger's plan was adopted by the federal government. Many city streets were paved by WPA-laid brick, though most have since been covered with asphalt; and four statues designed by Ellis Burman still stand as evidence of the joint sponsorships of the city and federal agencies. They are the War memorial in Antelope Park, the Pioneer Woman monument on Memorial Drive, the Smoke Signal at Pioneer Park, and the statue of Rebecca at the Well in the Sunken Garden.

The city was not considered out of the Depression until 1939; and some have thought that the war, and not federal projects, was what really brought the economy back to life. Two local histories, sponsored by the Federal Writers Project of the Works Progress Administration and the State of Nebraska, treat the Depression in just a bit over three paragraphs: the people were simply eager to get back to work and not dwell on the era's economic disasters.

For post office employees, getting back to work meant getting acquainted with a larger office building. In 1938 the federal government began the third section of the post office, virtually doubling the size of the existing structure, and moved the salt water fountain west, down the alley, to 9th

One of the first major carriers to serve the Lincoln Municipal Airport was United Airlines, one of whose airplanes is shown about to take off in February 1941.

Usual homecoming activities at the University of Nebraska include decorating the Greek houses. In October 1942, however, the students chose to forego traditional, frivolous paper decorations. "Scrap Homecoming" was part of a nationwide effort to collect metal and rubber for the World War II forces. Members of the university's Kappa Kappa Gamma sorority pose around their first-place homecoming "decorations."

Street. The artesian pressure was then insufficient and a pump had to be added, but salt water does not like to be pumped and the pipes and pump were soon corroded and abandoned. The post office, however, maintained the well, then under a manhole cover in the alley, in order to keep the "letter" of its promise to the city in 1873 when the government agreed to "drill a well and maintain it in perpetuity" for the city's citizens.

As the newly expanded post office opened in 1941, a committee was quietly looking over the Lincoln airport, which had just been enlarged through the efforts of a $10,000 Jaycee-sponsored bond drive. Within two months of the attack on Pearl Harbor, Lindbergh Field was chosen by the U.S. Army Air Corps as the site of a flight mechanics' school. In February 1942 Lieutenant Perly Lewis signed a 25-year lease with the city. The government then enlarged the 160-acre field, originally established in 1928, to nearly 3,000 acres, built more than 1,000 buildings, constructed four runways, and pumped $15 million into the local economy in less than six months. The nation and the city were at war.

E.J. Sias of Lincoln, an energetic young Christian minister who was somewhat of a local celebrity because of his amazing ability to raise funds and motivate his congregation, contributed to the training of pilots for the war effort. In 1910 Sias, convinced that the automobile was going to provide the dynamic base for a rapidly growing economy, established a mechanics' school known as the Lincoln Auto and Tractor School. With the advent of powered flight, he set his sight to the future and changed the name of his school to the Lincoln Airplane and Flying School and constructed a building to house it at 2145 O Street. In 1922 Charles Lindbergh became a student at the school and later brought it much prestige. The school itself was not only one of the oldest civilian aviation schools in the country but also held the highest rating given by the U.S. Bureau of Air Commission. In 1942 its name was changed to the Lincoln Aeronautical Institute. By the end of

World War II, the school's fleet of 14 aircraft had trained more than 3,500 men for the army air corps. When the war ended, so many pilots were thrown into the commercial market that there was no demand for further training and the school closed in 1947, a victim of its own success.

Under the guidance of Bennett Martin, Lincoln got its first war-related industry. Mr. Martin heard that the Elastic Stop-Nut Company of New Jersey was looking for an additional manufacturing site. When the land he hoped to interest them in near the present Sawyer-Snell Park proved to be under water, during a periodic Salt Creek flood, Martin showed the visiting manufacturers the then-empty Hebb Motor Works in Havelock. The foundations of this building, however, proved inadequate for the heavy machinery. Joe W. Seacrest then mentioned the availability of the block-long Union Terminal Merchandise Warehouse at 900 North 16th Street. The 330,000-square-foot building, later to house the Elgin Watch Company, still later to serve as the University of Nebraska's Nebraska Hall, soon had a labor force of 1,500 turning out millions of patented nuts and bolts. These fasteners were used by the thousands in every United States bomber because of a unique feature that caused them to not loosen under strain or vibration. The Hebb building was soon leased to and later purchased by the Goodyear Rubber Company, which manufactured puncture-proof rubber aircraft fuel tanks. Western Electric came to build telephone equipment for the army, and nearly a dozen local companies, including Cushman Motor Works and the Burlington Railroad, adapted their factories to war munitions and materiel.

Although the war effort spurred employment and industry, the Rudge and Guenzel department store, which had been operated by Allied Stores since the Depression, closed its profitable location at 13th and N as an offset against federal war excess profit taxation. Portions of the main floor and basement were then used as a USO facility. With the end of the war in 1945, many of the new firms, including

Above: A Huskerville resident is shown in 1947 paying for groceries. Huskerville was the community built around the Lincoln Air Base during World War II. After the war the base's barracks were used as housing for returning soldiers and their families. The community suffered an outbreak of polio in 1952 and closed down soon after that. Today the housing development of Air Park West sits on this land. Courtesy, University of Nebraska-Lincoln Archives

Opposite: Harry Hale, bartender for the American Legion Club, Omaha Post Number One, holds up an anti-Prohibition sign. Emotional debates stirred public sentiment on this statewide election issue, with Nebraska voting to end Prohibition in 1944. Courtesy, Journal-Star Publishing Company

Goodyear and Western Electric, stayed on, shifting to consumer and industrial production. Other operations, including Elastic Stop-Nut Company and the Lincoln Army Air Field, were closed by the end of the year. For a time the employment and economic picture was depressed, but through the efforts of the Chamber of Commerce and the "O Street Gang" businessmen, a whole new crop of business and government employers entered the city and ultimately broadened its economic base even more.

As the war came to an end, so did the era of the streetcar, whose days had been numbered since the introduction of buses in the 1920s. The interurban line proposed to connect Omaha, Lincoln, and Beatrice had given up the ghost on December 22, 1928. As the Japanese surrender was being signed aboard the U.S.S. *Missouri*, the College View (high) line, which had rattled down the center of Sheridan Boulevard since 1908 when the Woods brothers had installed it to enhance their residential home building along its right-of-way, ran its last car. The day of the bus had arrived.

During World War II the Lincoln Civic Singfest Committee sponsored Sunday evening programs on the north steps of the capitol. From this beginning and with

the guidance of the Women's Division of the Chamber of Commerce, Chet Ager's dream of nearly two decades earlier was realized with the construction of Pinewood Bowl. The funds for the 5,000-seat amphitheater were raised in 1945 and 1946, and it was officially dedicated in 1947. A bronze tablet near the entrance declares that the open-air auditorium was "erected to honor the heroic men and women of World War II, whose memory will live and grow, enduring forever."

In 1950 the Korean War prompted local efforts to reactivate the World War II air base, but the swift pace of construction experienced during its initial building was not again evidenced. A drive headed by the Chamber of Commerce raised nearly a half-million dollars to relocate Oak Creek, pave approaches, build a terminal, and lease Union Airport northeast of the city for general aviation usage. In June 1952 a 25-year joint-use lease was signed, and the Strategic Air Command formed two wings of B-47 bombers and refueling support teams as well as completing construction of numerous buildings and the seventh-longest runway in the world. After the war ended, on July 27, 1953, the base became headquarters for Atlas and Nike missile installations in the area. On June 1, 1966, the base was again deactivated and ownership transferred to the city of Lincoln under the direction of the Airport Authority Board.

A few days before the end of the Korean conflict, the Strauss Brothers Construction Company began building houses in Eastridge using their mass-construction concept. The Strausses, along with Peterson Construction Company and Witt and Juckette, built nearly 5,000 homes in the next three years, while Lincoln's population rose to more than 115,000.

The 1950s also saw the construction, at long last, of a new city auditorium. When the old auditorium burned down in 1928, it was hoped that a replacement would be built within a year. However, many obstacles arose. First, the question of title to the land at 13th and M could not readily be solved, and an alternative site

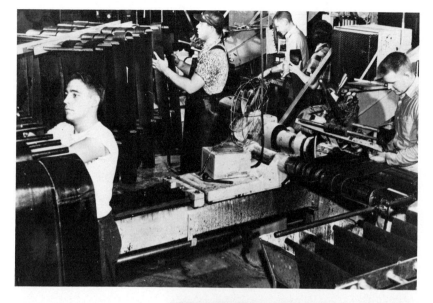

Above: The Goodyear Tire and Rubber Company received many military contracts during World War II. The Havelock plant has produced belts, puncture-proof fuel tanks, and tires for the military. Pictured in 1955, this plant has been enlarged a number of times and is still in operation. Courtesy, Journal-Star Printing Company

Right: Lincoln Telephone Company operator Evelyn Soukup demonstrates the outmoded method of placing a long distance call. The company began installing direct-dialing equipment soon after this 1953 photograph was taken. Courtesy, Journal-Star Printing Company

was sought. Through the efforts of the American Legion, on May 2, 1939, voters approved a $750,000 bond issue, but the bonds proved unsalable. In 1941 the old high school building and property at 15th and N were acquired for the project, but a group favoring location of the auditorium at 33rd and O streets tried in vain to have the voters determine the ultimate location. World War II intervened, putting a stop to the project. In 1949 the city's electorate approved an additional bond issue, providing a total of more than $2.5 million. With the Korean conflict, cost estimates continued to skyrocket, but the voters stood firm, resulting in a cutting back on the original plan, which called for a separate theater and sports arena, in favor of a single multipurpose building. Controversy over the location flared again, while postwar steel shortages further delayed construction. Finally, in April 1955, the city council approved the plans of Davis and Wilson Architects, and on May 4 excavation began at the 15th and N site. On April 23, 1956, the 300-pound cornerstone was set, and on March 10, 1957, the nearly 8,000-seat auditorium was officially opened. On May 24 the Kosmet Klub, the university's dramatic society, opened its production of *South Pacific*, just a few months short of 30 years after it closed *The Love Hater* in 1928.

Donald E. Thompson began working for the Burlington and Missouri River Railroad as a brakeman but rose to the position of Superintendent of the Western Division. Along the way he accumulated a fortune and, through a personal friendship with Theodore Roosevelt, founded the Lincoln *Star* in May 1902 with the primary goal of promoting Roosevelt's Presidential candidacy. After the election, Roosevelt showed his gratitude by appointing Thompson U.S. Ambassador to Brazil and later Mexico. In 1899 Thompson sold his home on the southwest corner of 15th and H to the state for $25,000. The house was first used as the official governor's mansion by William H. Poynter in 1899, who complained at having personally to pay upkeep on a house that was primarily a

THE UNIVERSITY OF NEBRASKA:
MORE THAN ACADEMICS FOR LINCOLN

Members of Alpha Omicron Phi hold a dance in the courtyard of their fraternity house in 1958. Courtesy, University of Nebraska-Lincoln Archives

In 1950 the enrollment at the University of Nebraska was 8,031— to the regents and administration, an uninspiring population. As the football team fell on hard times and a statewide clamor demanded a new coach, university officials decided to make the school into an exceptional institution. The regents came through with increased budgets for salaries and buildings, and the legislature confirmed their action by approving the measures. The '50s saw the rise of McCarthyism, with World War II anti-German feelings converted to anti-communism propaganda. The American Association of University Professors derided the witch-hunts; and the local faculty carefully watched the American Legion of Nebraska for attacks that never materialized. The student population, unconcerned with the political unrest surrounding Senator McCarthy, staged a panty raid in May 1952—the first time such an event was nationally publicized.

By 1960 the enrollment had risen by only 700, but the university faced turbulent times. The general populace of the state began questioning the university professors'

attacks on the status quo. They pointed out that their tax dollars were being used to create a generation of citizens who were attending college for the "purpose of eventually earning more than the average citizen" who didn't have a college degree. In 1961, the *Daily Nebraskan* editorially called for dissolving the House Un-American Activities Committee; the American Legion then publicly questioned the possibility of communism on campus.

The Nebraska press backed the rights of the students to dissent and question; and the administration assured the taxpayers of the loyalty of the university faculty and student body. Campus dissent then became more commonplace, as students discussed civil rights, ERA, Vietnam involvement, compulsory ROTC, and racism. And yet the Students for a Democratic Society (SDS) proved too liberal and failed to gain much support anywhere in the state. Throughout the '60s, students demanded and were accepted as partners in the academic community. The football team came alive in the national spotlight with the 1962 hiring of Bob Devaney as football coach. And by the end of the decade, enrollment soared to 19,618.

The university's impact on the Lincoln community has continually increased, with 1984 enrollment at 24,000 and a record 16,000 in the summer school programs. The university estimated that in 1984 its students and 8,000 employees would generate $309 million for the Lincoln trade area, $41 million in visitor spending, and contribute $6.5 million in local taxes. It is no surprise, then, that the university is often considered the largest employer and leading contributor of Lincoln's economy. As well it provides a cultural climate usually only associated with major metropolitan centers.

*Lance Corporal Richard
Lansing Zichek, 20, the
first Lincoln serviceman
to die in the Vietnam
War, was killed on July
15, 1965, while on sentry
duty near Da Nang Air
Base. He was buried in
Wyuka Cemetery with
full military honors.
Courtesy, Journal-Star
Printing Company*

Wyuka Cemetery at 36th and O streets holds an annual Memorial Day observance for those Lincoln residents who have died in battle. Courtesy, Journal-Star Printing Company

Above: In December 1955 a Navy jet fighter plane ran wild on the flight line and plunged into a hangar, starting the pictured blaze that killed three people (including the pilot) and destroyed seven aircraft. Accidents like this one led to cries for a base hospital, but none was ever built. Courtesy, Journal-Star Printing Company

Right: Audience members look at a display of stars at the State Museum Planetarium, located on the University of Nebraska-Lincoln campus. Funds for the planetarium, which opened in 1958, were provided by University of Nebraska alumnus Ralph Mueller. Courtesy, University of Nebraska-Lincoln Archives

state showplace. The mansion served through 19 governors (though Samuel R. McKelvie chose to remain in his own home on the northeast corner of 26th and N) until 1955, when the legislature authorized the construction of a replacement.

Governor Victor E. Anderson, elected in 1955, did not move into the official governor's residence. His wife, wary of the stove and furnace, permitted their son Roger to use the third-floor ballroom for his electric train while the family lived at their home in Havelock. In 1955 the legislature authorized construction of a new governor's mansion, and in 1958 the old residence was razed and the present building occupied. Some paneling and fixtures were reused in the new home, enabling Governor Anderson to use the same doorknob that Governor Poynter had used 58 years earlier. When Governor Ralph Brooks moved in the following year, his only publicly quoted impression of the mansion was that "the floors shake." This criticism was underscored by Bertram

Goodhue's architectural firm, which was shocked at the Selmer Solheim-designed red-brick mansion across the street from the stone-faced capitol. Local opinion won out, however, and the Old Virginian or Modified Georgian Colonial architecture has been accepted and praised by all its subsequent residents.

The year 1959 was chosen by the Lincoln Centennial Corporation as a point in time to look back at the desert land that had grown into a modern city of nearly 150,000, as well as a time to peer ahead into the future. Lincoln's centennial celebration began officially on May 2, 1959, with a parade of more than 100 floats, 35 marching bands, and 21 marching groups. That evening was the official centennial ball, called the White Lilac Ball, for a time when the capital city was nicknamed "The Lilac City." Along with Jan Garber's orchestra there was a two-hour stage show featuring George Gobel. The following eight Lincolnites were honored for their contributions to the city: George W. Holmes, finance; Robert E. Campbell, commerce; Oscar "Pop" Bennett, fine arts; Millard C. Lefler, education; Dr. J.E.M. Thomson, the professions; Fern Hubbard Orme, women's activities; Otto H. Liebers, agriculture; Dr. C. Vin White, religion.

During the week that followed, Dr. Walter Judd, congressman from Minnesota, spoke on Religious Heritage Day; Commerce and Industry Day spotlighted a number of local businessmen and saw the opening of a business exposition at the fairgrounds; "The Tower on the Plains," a pageant/history of Lincoln, starring Robert Culp, ran for five days at the Pershing Municipal Auditorium; Cultural Day featured street festivals downtown and in the suburbs; Historical Day honored local pioneer families; Youth Day had a dance at the University Coliseum starring Fabian; and a final parade on Western Day, along with a square-dance festival, brought the week to a close. Centennial Mall, which consisted of O Street closed from 11th to 13th streets and sodded and shaded with potted trees, lasted only through the summer. Fifty thousand "coins" good at

local merchants for 50 cents in trade till May 15, 1959, provided a more permanent memento of the celebration.

As it happened, 1959 was also the year that the Bankers' Life Insurance Company proposed building a major suburban shopping center northeast of its Cotner and O Street home office. The company's building proposal proved to be the start of an entire downtown-area reconstruction— by 1984 more than 75 percent of the city's retail sales would occur within a one-mile radius of the Gateway Shopping Center. As the population grew to 180,000 many other major building projects were proposed and completed. Between 1959 and 1984 downtown Lincoln witnessed profound changes.

Urban renewal was officially ushered in by the Nebraska legislature in 1969. With it came an intense period of revitalization and beautification for Lincoln. (This is evidenced citywide but is most dramatic in the downtown and Near South areas.) By 1970 a $171,000 downtown street lighting project was underway—the core beautification—which was to be complemented and reinforced by the Downtown Advisory Committee (DAC). In 1972 scramble pedestrian lights were experimented with and then, though the population liked them, were abandoned. Other ideas that were considered but never implemented were a tunnel under O Street, connecting Miller and Paine with the National Bank of Commerce, and the conversion of the old post office and city hall buildings into a civic and entertainment center. The successes included the completion of the Sheldon Memorial Art Gallery (1963), designed by Philip Johnson; the mirror-image twin Gere and Anderson branch libraries (1971), designed by Clark Enersen Partners; and the First National Bank and the National Bank of Commerce (1970), designed by I.M. Pei.

In 1975, under the administration of Mayor Sam Schwartzkopf, considerable interest in downtown redevelopment began. It was to be completed under Mayor Helen Boosalis, a strong advocate of the concept. During Mayor Boosalis' term,

Above: Civil rights demonstrators marched south on 13th Street toward the capitol on April 16, 1968. About 18 civil rights and religious groups in Lincoln participated in the silent protest. Courtesy, Journal-Star Printing Company

Left: The first warm weather of spring always brings thousands of winter-weary Lincolnites out to Pioneers Park to catch some sun and see the sights. Courtesy, Journal-Star Printing Company

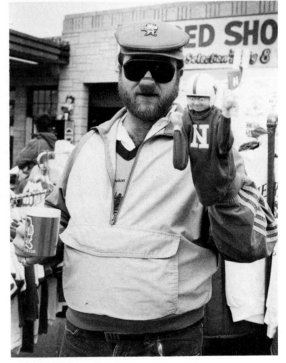

Left: The Haymarket district is currently seeing renovation. This section between 8th and 9th streets from P to Q streets is being developed into a number of shops, restaurants, and offices. Courtesy, Journal-Star Printing Company

Below: An employee of the Big Red Shop, 340 North 10th Street, is one of many vendors selling goods to fans on football Saturdays. Shoppers can buy everything from Big Red baby bottles to Big Red toilet seats. Photo by John Goecke

Above: Ervin Broman, a resident of Howard Trailer Court, stands among the cement animals that surround his home. Broman has made his "pets" for more than 30 years. Photo by Michelle Kubik

These five photos, taken less than a second apart, show the old Cornhusker Hotel being imploded on February 21, 1982. Thousands of Lincoln residents lined downtown streets as Controlled Demolition, Inc., brought the building to the ground in seconds. The hotel was razed to make way for the new Cornhusker Hotel and Convention Center, built by Los Angeles developer and financier David Murdock. Courtesy, Journal-Star Printing Company

Above: Students from Lincoln's Pershing and May Morley schools gather around Mayor Roland Luedtke in February 1984 as he signs a letter to include in a package destined for the Soviet city Akademgorodok. The package was meant as a gesture of good will. Luedtke, a former state senator and lieutenant governor, was elected Lincoln's current mayor in 1983. Courtesy, Journal-Star Printing Company

Bryan, Thomas Kennard, and William Ferguson homes. Also seeking to investigate and preserve Lincoln's history and heritage are the many neighborhood associations, Lincoln/Lancaster Landmarks, and the Lincoln/Lancaster Historical Society.

Although Lincoln's economy is being tested in the 1980s, the Prairie Capital has been tested many times before. Each time the village with "no water power, mines, fuel, nor other so-called natural advantages" has survived and grown stronger in the process. In just 125 years the village of Lancaster with 30 people in an area of less than half a square mile has become a city of 172,000 covering an area of just over 60,000 square miles. All of the elements that caused the development and prosperity of Lincoln are still vital and growing. The universities, governmental offices, the railroad, all are actively planning and paving the way for Lincoln's continued prosperity.

Left: This 1978 aerial view of a section of the University of Nebraska-Lincoln campus shows a portion of Memorial Football Stadium in the lower left. The stadium, built in 1926 to honor those men who died in World War I, seats about 76,000 fans, and every home game is a guaranteed sellout. Courtesy, George Tuck

Opposite page, bottom: The second anniversary of the Nebraska legislature's ratification of the Equal Rights Amendment was marked by a parade sponsored by the League of Women Voters of Lincoln, Lancaster County, and Nebraska. Courtesy, Journal-Star Printing Company

CHAPTER **VII**

PARTNERS IN PROGRESS

By Jack L. Kennedy

The Weiler Packing Company, on the west side of North 10th Street between P and Q, was opened between 1884 and 1888. The building, which still stands, is presently used for storage.

The past meets the present and prepares for the future in Lincoln.

It has been so for more than 100 years, for a people to whom conservativism means careful progress. There's no regressive reverence for the "Good Old Days," but there is a knowledge that without the past there would be no present and no future.

The *Lincoln Journal,* perhaps the city's oldest business, said more than a century ago that the city and state must develop transportation, water, education, and other resources. Lincoln has changed considerably since it got its election returns through a megaphone in front of the *Journal* offices at Ninth and P streets in the historic Haymarket area. The city is the home of a statewide public television network, which the Corporation for Public Broadcasting once termed one of the four best in the United States, producing nationally acclaimed and distributed programs. Touring ballet troupes have drawn crowds exceeded only by those in New York City. Few cities Lincoln's size can claim a major state university, two private colleges, and a large community college.

Political pioneers recognized long ago the virtues of a unicameral, non-partisan legislature. The skyscraper capitol, "The Tower on the Plains," might seem out of place to those who don't realize that Nebraskans are proud of progress, once the need is demonstrated. Megaphones gave way to computerized newspapers and electronic communication. The Haymarket

area itself has been restored, as harness factories became cafes, warehouses turned into nightclubs, and candy plants into office suites.

Businesses with foresight and a realistic view of how to build on the past converted former auto agencies and department stores into shops linked by a network of skywalks, as if to bridge the generation gap. The tree-lined streets downtown and in both new and mature residential areas soften the urban scene.

Rutted dirt roadways have long since given way to boulevards and to an interstate highway lined with modern sculptures, the state's bicentennial gift to the nation. College View, Havelock, Bethany, University Place, and other towns were once a long streetcar ride away from the capital, until community concern and foresight created one municipality.

That belief in the future caused early-day lawmakers to take the village of Lancaster; pass legislation designating specific sites for the seat of government, the home of the one state university, and the penal complex; rename the location Lincoln; and develop it into one of the nation's first planned cities, in which the past would be a guideline, not a barrier.

The organizations you will meet on the following pages have chosen to support this important civic event. They are representative of the businesses that have helped make Lincoln "The Prairie Capital" with the talent, skills, and determination that are the lifeblood of a thriving community.

135

LINCOLN-LANCASTER COUNTY HISTORICAL SOCIETY

From its origins as a small organization, born barely before the state's centennial, the Lincoln-Lancaster County Historical Society has become a catalyst for historic preservation in a variety of ways.

The Society initially set its sights on the need to preserve not only major structures, which deserved to be rescued from the wreckers, but the spirit of what the capital city and its environs has been, is now, and may become.

Founders of the Lincoln-Lancaster County Historical Society decided early on that its membership should be open to all who are interested in area history and in the preservation of the spirit as well as the structures that hold a key to the past, as well as furnish lessons for the future.

Early in 1964 a 10-member committee met with high hopes. It listed among its goals the hope to develop the preservation of written records of the city and county, increasing their availability to the public; the preservation of historic buildings, monuments, and markers; marking of historic sites; and commemorative anniversaries of historic events. Support of the then-approaching state centennial was another major motivation for the young, ambitious group.

On June 19, 1964, 20 people attended the Society's organizational meeting at Bennett Martin Library, and elected Mrs. Elinor L. Brown as president. She was to be a determined, driving force in the group's formative years.

The following year the organization sponsored "Century of Progress," a pictorial display of Lincoln and Lancaster County progress, drawn from the files of the State Historical Society and the *Lincoln Journal* and *Lincoln Star* libraries.

In the mid-1960s the Society began one of its major efforts—

Tenth and O streets looking east circa 1907. From the collection of William J. Wood.

saving the historic Kennard House. It was one of the first groups to realize the value of the home of Thomas P. Kennard, Nebraska's first secretary of state. The organization lobbied long and hard with legislators and others until the now beautifully restored landmark, with its changing seasonal displays, became the centerpiece of development for several other historic sites within view of the nationally known capitol.

The state's centennial found the Society staffing a sod house display on the capitol grounds, as well as sponsoring other events. The activities were a success, but Society leaders like Bill Wood, president in the 1980s, regret that some historic homes and other structures have slipped through their fingers.

Old City Hall circa 1912. From the collection of William J. Wood.

The organization was determined, however, to rescue one of the capital city's most historic structures, the Old City Hall, a former federal building and capstone of the revitalized downtown Haymarket area. With aid from a matching grant from the National Trust for Historic Preservation, the Society began a campaign to save the handsome structure. That drive succeeded, and major efforts to restore the building are a continuing project of the Society.

The Lincoln-Lancaster County Historical Society has also supplied historical articles for newspapers, held a dinner for families who have been on the farm for a century, and generally increased public awareness of the heritage of both Lincoln and Lancaster County.

NORDEN LABORATORIES

When Swedish immigrant Carl J. Norden, Sr., D.V.M., established a company in 1919 for the manufacture and sale of veterinary products, the hours were long and the work was hard. In the early years he often manufactured the products on weekends and sold them to veterinarians during the week.

What is today a nationally and internationally known leader in its field began in a second floor room at 144 North 10th Street, staffed by one office employee. By 1927 Norden Laboratories had moved to 227 North Ninth Street, where it occupied the entire first floor and where Norden did double duty, preparing both medications for animals and biological products for their immunization.

In 1934 Norden merged with Platte Valley Serum Company of Grand Island. Soon the new corporation occupied the entire building at 227 North Ninth Street, a nearby building on P Street, and a large farm and production plant in Grand Island. It also had four branch offices and eight distributors.

On January 8, 1954, after 35 years as president, Carl Norden became chairman of the board. Dr. E.C. Jones, former vice-president and

The Norden Laboratories plant and offices have been expanded several times in the past few decades and serve a worldwide veterinary clientele.

Dr. Carl Norden, Sr., sat proudly in a friend's buggy in the 1920s, ready to travel anywhere to sell his products.

sales manager, became president. Dr. Norden died seven months later.

In 1960 Norden Laboratories took a major step forward when it became a subsidiary of Smith Kline and French Laboratories. The firm's product line had grown to distribution through 26 U.S. branches and many foreign countries.

In the 1960s, under then-president Lewis E. Harris, Norden accomplished a major breakthrough in immunology by producing the first canine distemper vaccine utilizing a canine kidney stable cell line, which eliminated the need to grow the vaccine virus in living animals. The new vaccine proved to be both effective and safe, and its development helped elevate the firm's status in the industry. The

company also developed the first sustained-release medications for dogs and cattle.

To meet the increased sales, production, and research demands, Norden dedicated a new 182,000-square-foot plant on 137 acres at 601 West Cornhusker Highway in 1967. Two years later Dr. Jack Knappenberger became the firm's president and chairman of the board. At that time Norden had 305 employees and exported products to 34 countries.

George W. Ebright became president in 1976, and the firm soon introduced the first chewable tablet to control heartworm disease in dogs, the first vaccine to control pseudorabies in hogs, and a two-layered, sustained-release sulfamethazine tablet for cattle.

Dr. Norden's handsome horse-drawn cart has long since disappeared, but not his pioneering, inventive spirit. John P. Wareham became president in 1979, and in subsequent years expansion has continued. The plant has been enlarged four times since 1967, the company has 700 employees, and its products reach approximately 80 foreign countries. Norden Laboratories continues its research in an effort to help keep both pets and feed animals healthy and productive, the same goals a Swedish immigrant with a few ideas had at the turn of the century.

MILLER & PAINE

Miller & Paine, today on the corner of 13th and O streets, bears little resemblance to John E. Miller's original dry-goods business of the 1880s. But it is a living testimonial to his ability to envision the department store of the future.

In 1879, 21-year-old John E. Miller arrived in Lincoln, at the request of Captain J.W. Winger, to work in his dry-goods business. By 1883 J.E. Miller bought out Winger's interest completely in the 22- by 60-foot store.

Six years later Dr. B.L. Paine became a partner. He was never active in the business, and the Miller family purchased Paine's interest after his death. The store has been known as Miller & Paine since 1889.

A shrewd businessman, Miller forged on when others dared not, cutting prices and restocking shelves during the 1893 panic and borrowing from banks during the Panics of 1903 and 1907.

J.E. Miller died in 1938 at the age of 81, and his son, D.W. Miller, became president. The following year D.W. was killed in an airplane accident, and J.E. Miller's son-in-law, R.E. Campbell, became company president for the next 14 years.

R.E. Campbell was an innovator, installing Nebraska's first escalators.

In 1937 he erected an eight-story addition on O Street to the west, and farther west, a five-story structure for Ben Simon. In 1950 Miller & Paine built the JCPenney store, and, with another firm, constructed the Car Park building at 13th and M.

In 1953 R.E. Campbell was succeeded as president by his son, Brigadier General John Miller Campbell, a graduate from the University of Nebraska in business administration and recipient of the Air Force Distinguished Service Medal for military contributions.

Keeping pace with a mobile society, J.M. Campbell expanded

The original store as it is today, on the corner of 13th and O streets.

Miller & Paine into two shopping center locations: in 1964, at the Gateway Shopping Center in Lincoln, and in 1974, at the Conestoga Mall in Grand Island. Campbell was instrumental in the development of the Centrum and Skywalk projects, opened in October 1979, now connecting six blocks of retail business in downtown Lincoln.

Innovation continued. Inventory and purchase-order systems were totally computerized, and Miller & Paine was the first store in the country with an electronic system to automatically read price tags.

Today Robert E. Campbell II, John M. Campbell's son, serves as executive vice-president and merchandise manager. Carl B. Campbell, John's youngest son, is a student at the University of

Nebraska. Both stand by their father to continue the business built by their great-grandfather, J.E. Miller, on the belief that success comes from integrity and industry, a willingness to work hard, and a promise to always be fair to one's customers.

A new era in Nebraska retailing was begun in 1914 when Miller & Paine opened its new downtown store.

SECURITY MUTUAL LIFE NEBRASKA

Before the 20th century was born, a handful of Fremont, Nebraska, businessmen conceived the idea of forming an insurance company to provide security for the frontier's prairies. They started with little, but their goals were clear and simple; they wanted an economic shelter from loss. On October 3, 1895, Security Mutual Life Nebraska was born as a mutual benefit association, with little more than confidence as an asset.

The company's first president was R.B. Schneider, whose previous business interests included a local grain company, a bank, a railway company, and real estate. The first policyholder was Lucius D. Richards, who bought $1,000 worth of insurance from the fledgling firm's pioneer agent, A.G. Arnold.

The first year 279 members enrolled, and the firm soon outgrew its home in Fremont. In 1899 it moved to Lincoln, and in 1903 its charter was changed from a mutual benefit association to a mutual life company. With that, policyholders were granted, and continue to hold, ownership in Security Mutual Life.

When N.Z. Snell became president in 1906, a building was purchased in downtown Lincoln, at 12th and O streets. This location was the company's home office for more than 40 years.

The presidency of E.B. Stephenson spanned the devastating influenza epidemic of 1918, the prosperity of the 1920s, and the trials of the Great Depression's dust-bowl days, in an era when much of the firm's success depended upon agriculture. Security Mutual survived and provided cash-value loans, which helped save many small family farms.

In 1917 Ted Sick came to the company as a clerk. He would later become both president and chairman of the board, in an association that lasted 61 years. His 20-year presidency began in 1943 and spawned a period of growth. In 1947 the home office building was sold and temporary quarters were taken in Lincoln's Trust Building. Wartime employees who had their wages frozen were granted retroactive pay raises. In 1953 the company began to sell hospital and surgical insurance, and prosperity was again in the air.

Sick was also recognized as a leader in the industry. He was elected president of both the American Life Convention and the Life Insurance Association of America. It was also during his term as president of the firm that its present home office building was constructed on the Centennial Mall, as part of the planned park ribbon that would stretch from the capitol to the University of Nebraska-Lincoln.

In 1963 D.I. Parker succeeded Sick as president after 25 years with the company. He remained in office for nine years and was later elected chairman of the board.

When Leland Holdt became president in 1972, the company began a period of unequaled growth. From 1972 to 1982 life insurance in force increased by 253 percent. By the end of 1982 insurance in force exceeded three billion dollars. Assets had increased by 109 percent, and benefits paid to policyholders rose from $8.4 to $24.2 million.

The Fremont businessmen who founded Security Mutual Life Nebraska in 1895 were "at the center of a gathering destiny," one observer wrote later. That flowery optimism proved more truth than fiction, thanks to the growth of Lincoln, the state, and the area that Security Mutual serves.

The home office of Security Mutual Life Nebraska fronts the Centennial Mall's parkway ribbon, a symbol of the city's dedication to downtown redevelopment.

FIRST FEDERAL LINCOLN

Early in 1907 nine men with a vision of what Lincoln could become organized the Fidelity Savings and Loan Association in a basement.

Today's billion-dollar institution, First Federal Savings and Loan Association of Lincoln, has grown steadily from the commitment of A.R. Talbot, E.J. Hainer, C.E. Spangler, Dr. A.O. Faulkner, W.E. Sharp, T.S. Allen, H.B. Treat, and W.J. Hill, who served as directors, and W.A. Forsyth, who was elected president.

At first business was conducted in a rented room of the Fraternity Building, at the corner of 13th and N streets. By the end of the first year assets totaled approximately $13,000.

Fidelity continued to operate in its basement location until 1927, when the office moved to 223 South 13th Street. Changes were looming on the horizon, however, that would affect the fortunes of the entire nation. In 1929 the Great Depression hit, but Fidelity Savings and Loan weathered the storm and helped Lincoln survive.

As the 1930s saw the nation ease itself out of the Depression, sweeping changes came to the savings and loan industry. The years 1932 through 1934 brought the Federal Home Loan Act, the Home Owners' Loan Corporation, and insurance of accounts for savings and loan institutions.

In 1934 W.A. Forsyth was succeeded as president by his son, Evald M. Forsyth. Evald's wife, Gladys, who had been with Fidelity since 1929, became its secretary. By then the association's assets were .$300,000, and it was paying a dividend of one percent for savings.

An innovator from the beginning, Fidelity Savings and Loan was one of the first associations to apply for a federal charter under the Home

Longtime First Federal executive Gladys Forsyth fostered the firm's growth and was a widely recognized Lincoln civic leader.

Owners' Loan Act. In June 1935 it received its federal charter and insurance of accounts. Fidelity then

The home office of First Federal Savings and Loan Association, at 13th and N streets in downtown Lincoln, now serves more than 60 branches across the state.

changed its name to First Federal Savings and Loan Association of Lincoln, and was the first such organization in the city to offer insurance of savings.

In the years following, under the National Housing Act, which provided insurance of mortgages, First Federal became one of the first mortgage lenders to receive accreditation from the Federal Housing Administration and made the first FHA loan in Lincoln.

The 1940s were to be years of major expansion for the association, the savings and loan industry, and the city. With the end of World War II, First Federal saw the need for more housing as the city spread. It became the first mortgage lender in Nebraska to make veterans' loans.

By 1946 First Federal had grown to such an extent that a new building was needed, and the present home office was occupied at 1235 N Street. The following year, after the death of her husband, Gladys Forsyth became the association's third president.

It was impossible to separate Gladys Forsyth from First Federal. At a time when few women were leaders of financial institutions, she earned a national reputation. She was a world traveler, a renowned gardener whose home became a floral showplace, and a supporter of the University of Nebraska and any other enterprise that helped the capital city grow and mature.

Although by that time the institution had assets of more than six million dollars, Mrs. Forsyth always kept an eye open for likely spots in which to expand while at the same time showing concern for her employees. When she wasn't touring the state in search of new branches, she took a personal interest in such "fringe benefits" as the kitchen and dining room in the basement of the headquarters.

In 1954 First Federal opened its first branch, in Omaha. By the 1980s the association had 63 offices in 40 communities statewide. In the 1960s First Federal was the first financial institution in the nation to develop and implement money cards and electronic funds transfer for use in the savings and loan industry. The concept was the brainchild of John E. Dean, executive vice-president. In 1974 First Federal pioneered the use of remote terminals in grocery stores and other locations, which drew nationwide attention. Dean became president and Mrs. Forsyth chairman of the board in 1974. Two years later Charles H. Thorne was named president upon Dean's death. On

January 1, 1984, L.F. (Vern) Roschewski, an employee since 1956, was named president and chief operating officer. Thorne then became chairman of the board and chief executive officer. Gladys Forsyth died in March 1982, but the pace of First Federal's innovation and its concern for the prospective home owner have not diminished.

The team approach to management and the personalization that began when the 500-member staff was much smaller are credited with giving First Federal both an innovative edge and a low employee turnover. Both veterans and newcomers help Lincoln build for the next century. "First Federal," one employee boasted, "probably has more firsts than any other financial institution in the state." It's not unusual to find an employee of the

association who has been there for 25 or 30 years and remembers when the institution was initiating its expansion phase. As the financial needs of the state grew and Lincoln began to assert itself, First Federal absorbed six other savings and loans.

Taking a cue from the nine founders, Mrs. Forsyth, Dean, Thorne, and others, First Federal employees were encouraged to become active in their communities in a variety of roles. Financial transactions may be electronic now, but the association is still moved by its people.

Charles H. Thorne, chairman of the board and chief executive officer.

L.F. (Vern) Roschewski, president and chief operating officer.

WEAVER POTATO CHIPS

In 1932 Ed Weaver, Sr., was inspired by a cooker company advertisement expounding the benefits of the potato chip business. Unable to afford the equipment offered in the ad, Weaver set up a kettle on the family kitchen stove. Two years later production of the hand-scrubbed "Weavers Brownie Vitamin Chips" moved to the basement. Ed Weaver, Jr., a young boy when the business began, clearly remembers the smell of chips cooking that filled the house for the next decade.

The Weavers were in the potato chip business to stay, and the fledgling company began to expand its facilities, product line, and territory. It didn't take long to outgrow the basement.

In 1944 the company moved to a new plant at 129 South 21st Street, where the production of the renamed Weaver's Potato Wafers grew with the addition of a new continuous-line chip cooker. By 1950 the firm had moved to a more spacious facility at 610 L Street. Here production consumed 1,400 pounds of potatoes an hour. As Weaver's distribution stretched through Nebraska and the surrounding states, the plant expanded to eventually produce and process 5,000 pounds of Nebraska-grown potatoes per hour.

In 1964 another move brought Weaver's to its present location in the city's South Industrial Park. The new 45,000-square-foot facility was especially designed to handle future growth. From a beginning that featured only Weaver's Brownie Vitamin Chips, the firm now produces a variety of seasoned chips, fried cheese curls, and popcorn snacks. In June 1983 alone, a production record was set when over two million pounds of potatoes became Weaver Potato Chips.

New technology and new marketing techniques helped the company grow and mature, but the mainstay is still the potato. Eighty percent of the potatoes used come directly from local farms near Central City and Alliance. During the off season, potatoes are shipped from Arizona. Chipping potatoes are grown to a uniform, three-inch size and are high in starch but low in sugar.

After the potatoes are peeled and washed, each is inspected and trimmed before moving on to the slicer. Weaver's precision slicers control chip thickness to one ten-thousandth of an inch so all chips will emerge nearly uniform. From the slicer the potatoes ride through a revolving tumbler where the starch is literally washed from the surface of the chips. Next the slices pass under a patented spiked roller that puts the famous holes in the chips. These holes prevent blistering when they are being fried in a low-cholesterol vegetable cooking oil that has been especially prepared for the firm.

The carefully boxed products are then shipped to points in Nebraska, Kansas, Iowa, South Dakota, and Colorado. While the chips are the firm's best-known product, Weaver also uses about 5,000 pounds of Nebraska popcorn to make cheese corn and natural butter-flavored popcorn. A separate cheese curl and popcorn manufacturing area was added to the Lincoln plant in 1982 and an additional warehouse in 1984.

The family-owned business that grew from a basement, created Weaver's employee stock ownership plan, which allows employees to become stockholders in the company. Employees make no monetary contribution, but are awarded stock in relation to their normal compensation.

The firm moved to its present location in Lincoln's South Industrial Park in 1964.

WOODMEN ACCIDENT AND LIFE COMPANY

In 1890, Dr. A.O. Faulkner secured a charter from the State of Nebraska for Woodmen Accident and Life Company (originally called Modern Woodmen Accident Association), and launched the enterprise. He was a practicing physician in York, Nebraska, as well as the medical director of Modern Woodmen of America. He knew firsthand the need of people for protection against the financial losses of death and disability, and understood that what the individual would find difficult or impossible by himself could be accomplished for all if people joined together in an insurance company.

The company's first office was located in York, but in 1891, the headquarters was moved to Lincoln. After the relocation, Woodmen hired its first full-time employee. He was C.E. Spangler who, in his 51 years with the firm, served as secretary for 44 years, becoming chairman of the board in 1938, a position he held until his death in 1943.

For many years, Woodmen issued only policies of accident insurance providing benefits for loss of life, dismemberment, or disability. By 1916, however, it was apparent that complete disability protection required the addition of sickness insurance. Because the board of directors was conservative in its attitude toward what was then regarded as a hazardous type of underwriting, Central Health Company was organized as a running mate to write sickness-only insurance. In 1927, Dr. Faulkner, the firm's founder and the first president, passed away and was

succeeded by his eldest son, E.J. Faulkner, Sr. For all insurers, the Depression represented a period of extreme stress. But by diligent effort and conservative management, the companies worked their way through the Depression and emerged stronger than ever. In 1931, A.E. Faulkner succeeded to the presidency on the untimely death of his brother, E.J. Faulkner, Sr. In 1934, Woodmen amended its articles of incorporation to become a mutual legal reserve company, and two years later added life insurance and annuities to the coverage it offered. By the time of A.E. Faulkner's death in 1938, the pattern of the institution's future growth had been largely determined.

On September 1, 1938, E.J. Faulkner, Jr., was elected president and R.L. Spangler, executive vice-president. During Faulkner's military service in World War II, Spangler and W.S. Henrion, who would become senior vice-president and treasurer, guided the destiny of the organization.

The post-World War II period was one of significant growth and development. The expanding need for space in the home office demanded the construction of a new facility. A site opposite the state capitol was selected and the new building completed for occupancy in

1955. An addition to the home office was erected in 1970, more than doubling its size.

In 1977, the board of directors named E.J. Faulkner, chairman of the board, C.W. Faulkner, president, W.S. Henrion, vice-chairman, and John Haessler, executive vice-president, secretary, and general counsel. In 1984, C.W. Faulkner became chairman and chief executive officer and John Haessler president of Woodmen.

The success of Woodmen Accident and Life Company since 1890 is largely attributable to its adherence to the maxim of its founder, "The most of sound protection at reasonable cost."

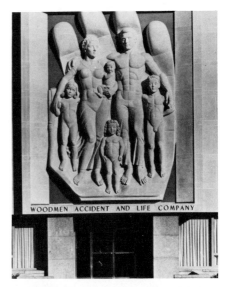

The home office of Woodmen Accident and Life Company (right), across from Nebraska's capitol, features "The Protecting Hand" sculpture (top right), which symbolizes society's basic unit—the family.

NOTIFIER COMPANY

Adventure into new and untried areas always fascinated Oliver T. Joy.

The University of Nebraska-Lincoln graduate was drawn to the challenges of South and Central America in the 1940s. He had been traveling up and down the Amazon for 25 years doing geological research when an acquaintance told him about a slightly less dangerous idea he had developed—a new thermostat.

Joy had a lot of time to think about the invention while in the jungles, and he reached a conclusion. He left the Amazon in 1949 to begin the development of Notifier Fire Alarms with a friend in a tiny office-like cubicle on Highway 6 in Waverly.

As both the plant and his ideas grew, a factory was established in downtown Lincoln at 239 South 11th Street. It wasn't long before his staff had grown to some 35 people. He was assisted by his wife, Dr. Margaret O. Joy, as executive vice-president, who later became the only woman in the fire protection industry to appear in "Who's Who in American Women."

In April 1959, 6.5 acres were acquired in northeast Lincoln, and a 12,000-square-foot plant and office structure was built at 3700 North 56th Street. Within the next seven years a total of 25,000 square feet were gradually added. Notifier was the first Midwest manufacturing plant to be completely air conditioned. The company currently covers 75,000 square feet.

In January 1968 Joy sold the business and assets of Notifier Corporation to Emhart Corporation, a diversified worldwide Fortune 500 company. Paul F. Walker was named vice-president and general manager. The trade name was Notifier Company, a subsidiary of Emhart.

In February 1969 Joseph P. Ferrara was named president and general manager. The plant soon began making the 911 smoke detector—Notifier's first entry into the expanding consumer market. More products were added to the commercial line, including a multizone solid-state fire control panel and a two-wired ionization detector.

Calvin B. Mortensen became the present and general manager in June 1979. In August 1981 Robert H. Baldwin was named vice-president and general manager.

Notifier Company has come a long way since its inception. The firm, which began installing its product in a few nursing homes and hospitals within a 100-mile radius of Lincoln, now provides protection to such industrial giants as Ford Motor Company, General Motors, IBM, Bendix Corporation, and the Smithsonian Institution.

During more than a quarter-century of designing, manufacturing, and marketing fire alarm, detection, and security equipment, Notifier Company has earned an enviable reputation for its ability to combine innovation with solid, practical engineering. In addition, Notifier has pioneered many of the concepts used today, including the use of low-voltage and modular panels.

Notifier Company is in the life safety and security communication business, including sensing, signaling, transmission, and control for fire protection and prevention, primarily in small to medium-size commercial buildings.

These products are used in the automated fire detection systems market and the automatic sprinkler systems market, and are sold primarily through a channel of independent distributors.

A unique product Notifier sells is a waterflow detector, which serves the automatic sprinkler systems market. Notifier enjoys approximately 60 per cent of this particular market. This product, along with certain unique applications of various panels, allows Notifier to bid and obtain certain specific jobs and sell its other devices.

The consumer line consists of light commercial and residential security systems.

The firm, which began with two men and an idea nurtured during an Amazon expedition, has grown to a multinational business, with 175 employees, whose products are sold on a worldwide basis.

Notifier Company is located at 3700 North 56th Street, Lincoln.

KNUDSEN, BERKHEIMER, RICHARDSON & ENDACOTT

In 1981 Knudsen, Berkheimer, Richardson & Endacott commemorated 100 years of service to Lincoln and the legal profession with the visit of the Chief Justice of the United States, Warren Burger. When Jesse B. Strode hung out his shingle in 1881, he could not have foreseen the changes that would occur in his law firm in its first century.

Strode and his first partners, Edmund C. Strode and Jesse L. Root, made an early commitment to public service. Jesse Strode became the county attorney and later a district judge. Ed Strode was city attorney from 1907 to 1910, and Root assisted the Supreme Court of Nebraska.

Max Beghtol was senior partner in 1928, when the firm moved its offices to the newly constructed Stuart Building. There it assembled a law library that was larger than the Nebraska State Law Library.

The firm diversified as it grew, representing a variety of new clients, including local businesses, railroads, banks, and insurance companies. (Not all prospective clients were accepted, however. Beghtol declined the business of an emissary of John Dillinger whose shoulder holster bulged beneath his suitcoat.)

In 1908 retired Judge Edward P. Holmes had founded another law firm, which ultimately became Chambers, Holland, Dudgeon & Beam. In 1971 the two firms merged, becoming Knudsen, Berkheimer, Endacott & Beam.

In 1976 the firm became one of the first tenants in the new NBC Center, designed by architect I.M. Pei, where its 21 lawyers now office.

Knudsen, Berkheimer, Richardson & Endacott is known for its work in personal injury and commercial litigation, banking, probate and estate planning, and real estate. Its members have also been active in government, from the days when the firm represented Governor Sam McKelvie to the service of former partner John Mason on the Lincoln City Council and its current representation before the state legislature and other governmental agencies for a variety of clients, including the Nebraska State Bar Association.

Knudsen, Berkheimer maintains the commitment to public service begun by its founders. J. Lee Rankin left the firm to serve as Solicitor General of the United States from 1956 to 1961 and later as General Counsel to the Warren Commission, which investigated the assassination of John F. Kennedy. Former partners now in the judiciary include William C. Hastings, Nebraska Supreme Court; Donald E. Endacott, state district judge; and C. Arlen Beam, U.S. district judge. Current partner Richard Berkheimer served as a member of the Commission of Industrial Relations.

Dedication to professional excellence is expressed by participation in the activities of the American, Nebraska, and Lincoln Bar associations, and the UNL College of Law. (Senior partner Richard A. Knudsen served as president of the Lincoln and Nebraska State Bar associations.) Lawyers in the firm continue to serve the community in many civic, cultural, and political organizations, such as the Lincoln Foundation, the Community Playhouse, Children's Zoo, the Nebraska Arts Council, Bryan Memorial Hospital, the Cooper Foundation, Sheldon Art Gallery, Food Bank, the YMCA, and Lincoln General Hospital.

The lawyers and staff of Knudsen, Berkheimer, Richardson & Endacott, remembering their heritage, look forward to a second century of commitment to the practice of law and service to the community.

Chief Justice Warren Burger (left) and Richard Knudsen prepare for Burger's address marking the firm's centennial.

BACK TO THE BIBLE BROADCAST

Theodore and Matilda Epp, founders of the Back to the Bible Broadcast.

Back to the Bible Broadcast, a worldwide radio ministry, receives more than a half-million pieces of mail a year from all over the world.

A 1945 production of youth broadcast (left to right): Mrs. Melvin Jones, Viola Ortegren, Mrs. Theodore Epp (ladies trio); Anna Marie Eavey, organist; the Epp children, Herbert, Berniece, Marilyn, and Eleanor; Thelma Donaldson, pianist; Theodore Epp; and Melvin Jones.

The program's 5,951 broadcasts a week worldwide, as well as Bible study courses, publications, counseling, and other services, represent a commitment to reaching others with Christ's message.

The ministry was started in the 1930s by the Reverend Theodore Epp, a Southwest Baptist Seminary graduate who once considered being a missionary to Russia. He began by helping an Oklahoma minister on his radio broadcasts. The ministry was successful, but something kept nagging at Epp. Sometimes, he said, "God prepares his servant to move on."

In the fall of 1938 the Epps visited his parents in Nebraska. During his stay, a young woman

Male quartet, 1945 (left to right): Theodore Epp, Darrel Handel, Ernest Lott, and Melvin Jones.

suggested to him that he start a daily gospel broadcast in Nebraska. Epp tried to dismiss the idea from his mind, but couldn't. He'd been offered a pastorate in Kansas and been invited to be a penitentiary

chaplain. He even rented a home in Kansas and prepared to move, but something told him to take another road.

In May 1939 he walked into a radio station in Lincoln, alone, with $65 that he had been given to start the new radio ministry. He'd budgeted carefully. That was enough to pay for time on the small station for three weeks, leaving $30 to live on, half of which went for room rent. Meal money was rationed at 50 cents a day. The family moved to Lincoln the next month. His wife was reassuring, but the bank account wasn't. However, God met the needs day by day.

At that time, the organization didn't have sophisticated studios, its own production staff, or the international arms it does today. It didn't have more than 1,000 radio stations releasing the programs, 107 on a Spanish network alone.

What it did have was Theodore Epp's faith that God would provide and his belief that many people needed the intimate approach he tried to achieve through his early broadcasts. He prepared the broadcasts and conducted business from the study of his home, at 19th and R streets. In 1940 Epp decided to move to Grand Island and work out of the basement of his home while broadcasting on pioneer radio station KMMJ.

In 1942 Epp saw an opportunity to broadcast on the powerful KFAB, then located in Lincoln. Back to the Bible headquarters was moved back to Lincoln and the office was located at 27th and Sumner streets. That same year, the first issue of the magazine that is now the *Good News Broadcaster* was published. The following year the fledgling enterprise entered a new phase of its life—shortwave transmission.

The program was first released over shortwave from missionary radio station HCJB in Quito, Ecuador. In 1960 TWR-Monte Carlo began operations and released the broadcast. By 1971 engineers had developed a new antenna to produce a stronger shortwave signal into Great Britain.

In 1944 the first home Bible study course from Back to the Bible was completed. The *Good News Broadcaster* became a monthly gospel newspaper. In February 1946 the first youth magazine, *Young America,* (now *Young Ambassador),* was published to accent the role youth have always played in the broadcasts.

In the early days there was no music on the program. Before long, the Epps were half of a quartet. They were joined by Mr. and Mrs. Melvin Jones. Jones, Epp's first employee, helped with the mail, filing, and bookkeeping. They knew they had to reach the youth, and soon the three oldest Epp children began singing on the programs.

Back to the Bible, which now has about 230 employees in Lincoln and about 175 outside the United States, moved its headquarters to the Terminal Building downtown in 1943. Then, for five years, they operated out of quarters over a soft-drink bottling plant at 24th and O streets.

In 1952 the growing enterprise moved to a refurbished building near the Cornhusker Hotel, the former home of the *Lincoln Star* newspaper. It was renamed the Good News Building.

The pace of activities quickened at 12th and M streets. G. Christian Weiss joined the staff as the Voice of Foreign Missions, and missionary programs became a regular part of the weekly broadcast schedule. Between January 1954 and October 1958 branch offices were opened in Canada, England, Sri Lanka (then Ceylon), the Philippines, Australia,

Melvin Jones, Dr. Epp's first employee and still an executive with the organization, was business manager and mail delivery person when this photo was taken in 1945.

and Jamaica. An Italian broadcast began in 1961.

Epp and Jones readily point out that all of the overseas offices, are operated and controlled by local residents. Each has its own board and management personnel. That approach has helped the Americans overcome any hint of colonialism, Jones says. The overseas programs are now heard in nine languages, ranging from Hindi to Spanish.

Back to the Bible helps sponsor 22 other foreign-language programs, as well as programs beamed to mainland China by the Far East Broadcasting Company. Some 270 individual missionaries are partially supported with money sent in by

Dr. Epp in 1948, producing a program in his study.

listeners.

In many cases leaders of other nations were willing to allow the Back to the Bible message on the air because it was nonpolitical. That is a credo Epp has followed since his earliest days as an Oklahoma broadcaster. Epp believes that Christ carries the message through him; therefore, Back to the Bible is not a one-man or "family" operation.

Epp was one of the founders of the National Religious Broadcasters Association in the 1940s, and its board members still consider him "their conscience." They still ask, "What would Dr. Epp say about that?"

A fire in the printshop on O Street in 1951 caused only a slight delay in Back to the Bible's international ministry, which reaches millions of homes over 1,000 radio stations.

On January 15, 1980, the Back to the Bible Broadcast was accepted as a charter member of the new Evangelical Council for Financial Accountability. The council is a self-governing association of Christian organizations that are committed to strict compliance with stated standards of financial disclosure and accountability. The

The Lincoln Star newspaper building, renamed the Good News Building, 1952.

Radio speakers of the early 1960s (left to right): Dr. G. Christian Weiss, the Reverend Ord Morrow, and Dr. Theodore Epp.

group sets rigorous standards for members and interprets the position of evangelical organizations before

the U.S. government when asked.

Although listeners around the world think of Back to the Bible as an inspirational radio program, it also publishes popular correspondence courses and books, Bible studies, booklets on Christian living, character studies of important biblical people, fiction for teenagers, large-print books for the visually impaired, and a variety of Christian songbooks, choir arrangements, cantatas, and recordings.

Back to the Bible has considered the possibility of going into television, but Epp likes the unique qualities of radio and the emphasis on the message rather than on what some see as showmanship. Radio, he believes, is a personal friend, a more intimate tool, a more economical way to reach into all corners of the world.

The organization has a budget of about $10 million, with another $4 million for worldwide operations. Back to the Bible is still expanding and has constructed several new overseas offices and radio studios in recent years. It began an in-house radio agency, Good Life Associates, in 1982.

Epp is thankful for the transistor radio, which has helped take the programs into even more remote locations than were possible when the apprehensive young preacher from Oklahoma walked into the small Lincoln station in 1939.

He is no longer concerned about where the next $65 will come from to purchase broadcast time, or if the printshop will be hit by a flood and then a fire. He is concerned about reaching out to more people in more countries and is determined to do it even if it takes a hand-cranked cassette tape recorder for homes without electricity, as Back to the Bible has provided in some countries. He'll continue to broadcast the "Good News."

VALENTINO'S

It was clear to Val and Zena Weiler by 1957 that the Campus Fruit Market they operated, across from the east campus of the University of Nebraska-Lincoln was soon going to be eclipsed by the rush of new supermarkets that dotted the city.

The landmark, which had stood for a dozen years, had to go. In its place, armed with three dozen pizza pans, a recipe that had been in Mrs. Weiler's family for years, and a generous amount of trepidation, they decided to open a pizza business.

They didn't advertise the opening on that hot July day, but, they took in $60 anyway.

As the establishment's reputation grew, patrons watched through a window as the pizza was being made. Customers waited for an hour or more, in line or in the crowded restaurant, to sample the pizza or other Italian specialties that Val and Zena concocted. Zena's recipe was a secret—and it still is. The pizza is made in the restaurants just as carefully as expansion plans are made in the boardroom. Valentino's now includes 30 franchised and company-owned restaurants in Lincoln and Omaha, plus others ranging from North Dakota to Texas and from New Mexico to Ohio. Expansion is by design, not by chance, to protect the quality of the product.

To many of Val's customers, being in a city without a Valentino's pizza is as bad as being caught without a University of Nebraska season football ticket. That hasn't stopped the devoted customers from getting their favorite food, however. Val's has shipped pizza to every corner of the continental United States, to university alumni gatherings in Washington, D.C., to hungry and nostalgic ex-collegians in Arizona who want a delectable Christmas present, as well as to Alaska and

The original Valentino's, at 35th and Holdrege streets, prior to it being enlarged and remodeled.

Japan. If necessary, the firm will send someone along to make sure the pizza is handled and served properly. Visitors to Lincoln have ordered their pizza packed in dry ice so they can take it home with them.

The company-owned restaurants alone make 40,000 pizzas a week. But, as Valentino's has grown, it hasn't lost Val and Zena's passion for perfection, cleanliness, and friendly service.

In 1971 the Weilers sold the restaurant to Tony and Ron Messineo. However, all that changed was the family name. As the firm expanded, so did the menu. The decor was enhanced to create a full-service family atmosphere, but old standbys remained. The separate take-out business Val and Zena started is still strong. In fact, the original store sold 7,200 pizzas on one cold basketball Saturday. Valentino's still operates by a written corporate creed that says that community service is as important as the quality of the food, and employees have been active in many civic causes.

In 1984 the firm moved its corporate offices from the Terminal Building in downtown Lincoln to new quarters a few blocks away in the city's historic Haymarket area.

Somehow, the move seemed

appropriate for the Campus Fruit Market, which had become a nationally known, carefully grown Italian restaurant chain. Valentino's now has thousands of employees who are pledged to keep Zena's delicious secret—and her high standards.

One of Valentino's Omaha restaurants features a beautifully restored tin ceiling and an inviting atmosphere.

LINCOLN TELEPHONE AND TELEGRAPH COMPANY

The Lincoln Telephone and Telegraph Company, born to battle the giants in 1903 when the industry itself was an infant, lost no time in proving it was a fiesty child, aiming for success. From its beginning to the present, LT&T has introduced a number of "firsts" in Nebraska's telephone industry.

For example, in 1904 the young company made the first successful dial installation in the state. In 1946 it offered the first radio-telephone service, and four years later LT&T had the first dial toll center in the state designed for connection with the nationwide toll dialing system.

LT&T offered the first direct-distance dialing in the state, in Beatrice in 1957. In 1960 the first coast-to-coast direct-distance dialing in Nebraska became available over its network.

As technology brought people closer together, LT&T pioneered the first experimental in-WATS (Wide Area Telephone Service) in the nation. The first intra-state in-WATS followed in 1968, as did the first 911 emergency service in the state. By 1971 the company had opened the first electronically controlled exchange in Nebraska, at Waverly.

New technology now carries telephone messages via fiber optics. As telephone poles in rural areas faded into history and voice transmission went underground, LT&T installed Nebraska's first fiber optic telecommunications link. The new glass cable uses a laser light the size of a grain of salt to transmit voice, data, and video communications. Each tiny pair of fibers can carry over 8,000 voice communications.

To meet the growing needs of the information age, LT&T offered Nebraskans a data communications network, PrairieLink™, in 1984. This network allows customers to send large volumes of data from one place to another without having to go through complicated format changes when computers are not compatible.

To the layperson the new technology may seem an impossible puzzle, just like the one many thought Frank H. Woods faced in 1903.

Woods, tagged "the great independent" by the head of AT&T, the largest U.S. phone company, fought for decades with grit and determination for what he believed was the best approach to fairness and good service for the 22-county area served by LT&T. Yet, it was almost by chance that Woods took an interest in what was to become LT&T.

In 1903 Charles Bills and his brother, Frank, started a telephone company in Lincoln called the Western Union Independent Telephone Company, which was to operate in direct competition with the firmly established Bell exchange

The Lincoln Telephone and Telegraph Company's downtown headquarters at 14th and M streets serves a 22-county southeast Nebraska area with a variety of telecommunications capabilities. Engineering, shop, and garage/warehouse facilities are also in Lincoln.

The company's equipment has undergone a radical change to computer use and fiber-optic cables since this 1960 crew of operators was busy in the Lincoln headquarters building.

that had opened about 1880. The Bills brothers sought the legal assistance of Woods, then 35 years old and a member of the Lincoln law firm of Hall, Woods and Pound.

On May 4, 1903, the seven original stockholders, including Woods and his brothers, Mark and George, held their first meeting. In June 1904 the new venture, now called the Lincoln Telephone Company, began to serve customers with a newfangled Strowger automatic dial system. The entire industry, both independent and Bell, turned toward the company to see if the new device would work.

In 1905, when Woods became president, he realized that the independent phone companies could not long continue the strife with Bell. In December 1909, when the controversy over interconnection was at its peak, he attended the convention of the National Independent Telephone Association and was elected president. He promptly set about to rectify the enormous problems facing the telephone industry.

Woods announced he was in favor of physical interconnection with the Bell system and other independents. He thought he had an ally in Henry P. Davidson, a partner of banking magnate J.P. Morgan who had taken over several Ohio telephone properties.

Although Morgan had financial ties with the Bell system, Davidson announced in 1909 that they were in the independent ranks. Davidson also said he, like Woods, wanted to end the competition that was stifling the development of a public network.

Woods chaired a committee named to negotiate with Bell. For two years there was talk about the need to give the public better service and to eliminate the costly and inefficient competition that resulted when independents and Bell had rival systems in the same town.

The negotiations faltered more than once. At one point Davidson, under persistent questioning, tried to hide the Bell ties. This outraged

Lacking today's modern technology, telephone workmen used plenty of horsepower around the turn of the century as construction began on a new telephone company addition in downtown Lincoln.

The growing firm's business office in Lincoln was crowded but efficient in 1909.

Woods, who stormed out of the room. Other independents urged him to return and apologize to Davidson, to which Woods thundered: "You go back in there and tell him and the rest of them to go plumb to hell!"

The next morning Davidson awakened Woods with a telephone call, telling him that the president of AT&T wanted to see him. The mountain had come to Mohammed, and Theodore Vail and Frank Woods soon found that they were both direct, logical, and determined to find a way to serve the public interest.

On January 8, 1912, LT&T's board of directors put its stamp of approval on an agreement for the purchase of the Bell properties in 22 southeast Nebraska counties. Woods had won his battle with the giant. For years he had over his office desk a picture of Vail inscribed, "to the great independent, from his friend, Theo. N. Vail."

LT&T prospered under Woods' leadership until his death in 1952 and later under that of his sons. Frank Woods, Jr., who as a boy accompanied his father on trips east to negotiate with Bell, served as

chairman of the board and Thomas C. Woods, Sr., as president.

By the 1980s the firm "the great independent" founded had become the 17th-largest telephone company in the nation and is still growing with Thomas C. Woods, Jr., as chairman of the board and chief executive officer. The corporation has more than 1,700 employees serving 174,000 customers in 185 towns through 137 exchanges.

As the forces of deregulation and technological advances began to alter the structure of the industry again in the late 1970s, LT&T was reorganized and became the major subsidiary of the Lincoln Telecommunications Company (LinTelcom) in 1981. Thomas C. Woods III, a vice-president of LinTelcom, heads the three new subsidiaries which market telecommunication equipment, supplies, and special services.

Woods and other company officials throughout southeast Nebraska have always contributed to many community projects and charitable causes. To the area covered by LT&T, service means much more than a friendly voice on the phone or a cable able to carry calls with the speed of light. It also means a corporate commitment to the region of which it is a part.

DAVIS/FENTON/STANGE/DARLING
ARCHITECTS/ENGINEERS/INTERIOR DESIGNERS

Davis/Fenton/Stange/Darling
Architects/Engineers/Interior Designers
live in a landmark they designed
and create new ones virtually every
day across Lincoln and much of
Nebraska.

The office/theater skyscraper that
has dominated the corner of 13th
and P streets for more than 50 years
was the first building of its type
which the city had seen. The
architecture was eclectic, blending
the styles of the day. Newspapers
hailed it as a monument to the
progress of a greater Lincoln.

The firm has the same philosophy
and vision today. It has broadened
to help Lincoln and other cities
preserve the best of the old, not
merely design new Stuarts or high
schools or department stores.

Ellery L. Davis graduated from
Columbia University in 1908 with a
degree in architecture. He worked as
a draftsman in Lincoln for a time,
then in 1911 formed a partnership
with George Berlinghof and secured
the commission to design the new
Lincoln High School at 22nd and J

The design for Lincoln General Hospital
broke new ground in nursing unit
configuration with its pod system. The
project was honored with state A.I.A. design
awards and highlighted in several
publications.

The Stuart Building, shown here in the 1940s,
has been a downtown Lincoln anchor since
1927 when it was designed by Davis/
Fenton/Stange/Darling. Its longtime tenants
include the architectural firm.

streets. Also included in this
commission was the development of
the new Bancroft Elementary School
at 14th and Vine streets, later a part
of the University of Nebraska.

The Miller & Paine Department
Store was the firm's next major
project in 1914. It shows many of
the same architectural considerations
as the high school building that
began Davis' career.

Davis separated from Berlinghof
in 1915. In 1921 Walter F. Wilson
joined the firm but the largely
agricultural area didn't provide
enough opportunities for the
ambitious partners, so they began
reaching across the state—even
when a passing farmer had to bring
a team of horses to extract their car
from the mud.

During the 1920s the firm was
extremely active as the city grew.

The partners designed the
University of Nebraska football
stadium, the Stuart, and several
buildings at the university, where
Davis had taught mathematics
during the lean years until the
armistice that ended World War I.

Ellery H. Davis joined the firm
after the completion of his collegiate
work at Columbia University and
the University of Nebraska in 1936.

During the 1940s the concern bid
for and won a contract for a
$20-million air base outside of
Denver that included everything
from schools to the base fire station.
At the peak of this operation, the
firm employed some 300 people.

The early postwar years brought
expansion into school buildings,
hospitals, and other projects,
meaning more time on the road.
Davis carried with him a 100-watt
light bulb as a temporary
replacement for the 20-watt bulb he
often found in small hotels, so he
could see to read.

In the 1940s and 1950s the
partners designed Southeast High

The East Junior-Senior High School complex, which won national recognition, was designed by Davis/Fenton/Stange/Darling to take advantage of the need for open space and dual use for adult classes.

School and the Hastings College Chapel, as well as more university structures and hospitals. In 1962 the firm received national attention for its design of the new East High School, with such innovations as flexible spaces and provisions for both television and year-round use. That same year its Dorsey Laboratories design was chosen as one of the top 10 plants of the year by *Factory* magazine.

In 1962 Bill Fenton and Jim Stange were named stockholders and principals in the firm. Stange's primary responsibilities were in design and client relations. In 1967 Pat Darling, a mechanical engineer and University of Nebraska graduate, became a stockholder and the name was changed to Davis/Fenton/Stange/Darling.

From two principals and about 20 professionals, DFSD has grown into a firm with four principals and 41 professionals. When Davis retired in 1977 Stange was elected president and chairman of the board. Fenton, Darling, and Lynn Jones are

vice-presidents. Stange, Fenton, and Jones have each been president of the state society of the American Institute of Architects.

As the firm drew Lincoln into the 1970s and 1980s, it was asked to design the remodeling of its original project, Lincoln High School, at a cost of more than one million dollars. The project won a national award from the American Association of School Administrators for its color, open space, and creative approach to making an older building come alive.

Such preservation projects are more on the minds of Americans today, as they rediscover the value of their landmarks. In some cases, Stange says, the firm has "rehabilitated spaces that were badly tortured by somebody else." In other cases, in cooperation with other architects, DFSD designed Pershing Municipal Auditorium and the Lincoln Airport Terminal to fit new uses for a new day. The firm is now multidisciplined. It offers architecture and engineering services as well as interior design expertise and can even design furnishings that fit into the total environment.

Architectural tastes and approaches tend to be somewhat cyclical but the firm has not lost

The Nebraska Wesleyan University Theater and Speech Center serves both the university and the Lincoln community. The design was honored nationally for its angularity, simplicity, use of color, and energy efficiency.

sight of Davis' original commitment to designs that will endure. The firm is "modernist," Stange says, but "within the context of our region and community." It does not bow to any single architectural school.

The 1980s made new demands on the diverse firm as the nation began to look at how to conserve its heritage and its resources, as well as how to make downtown areas come alive again.

In 1980 DFSD designed a new YMCA for Hastings, as a sign of rising interest in physical fitness. Then came Lincoln's downtown Skywalk system to link several major structures, which brings forth an entirely new theory of retail development and preservation of the city's core.

Other important recent projects include the expansion of Bryan and Lincoln General hospitals, the NBC Center in association with I.M Pei, and a fieldhouse and theater center for Nebraska Wesleyan University.

"I had to restrain my enthusiasm for Mies Van Der Rohe, Frank Lloyd Wright, and Le Corbusier. Our clients had not yet heard of the international style. They wanted, and got, Georgian," Ellery Hall Davis, son of the founder, said when he joined the firm during the Depression.

Today clients of Davis/Fenton/ Stange/Darling, expect—and receive—diversified integrated services from the broad-based design enterprise.

NEBCO, INC.

NEBCO, Inc., and their antecedents have been paving the way for growth in Nebraska since 1908, the year George P. Abel and Charles Roberts, University of Nebraska engineering graduates, originally did sewer work for the Burlington Railroad in Nebraska.

In 1910, when the capital was still young, Abel and Roberts did their first city paving project, a segment of O Street from 33rd east to Wyuka Cemetery.

As the volume of business grew, the partnership was dissolved in 1915, and two new ventures, Abel Construction Company and Roberts Construction Company, were formed. George Abel opened his first business office in 1916, moving it out of his home. In December of that year he married Hazel Hempel. She was to become a strong figure in the community, becoming the first woman in Nebraska to be elected to the United States Senate in 1954, and was named American Mother of the Year in 1957.

As the firm's reputation and needs grew, Abel and Charles Roberts jointly purchased the Buffalo Brick Company of Buffalo, Kansas.

In 1928 Abel purchased the defunct and bankrupt Omaha, Lincoln and Beatrice Railway Company and converted the interurban railway into a switching terminal railroad. In 1930 Abel and Charles Stuart built the Union Terminal warehouse at 17th and Avery streets, now Nebraska Hall on the University of Nebraska-Lincoln campus.

Abel opened one of the United States' first ready-mix concrete plants in 1929. General Steel Products Company was founded in 1934 to manufacture concrete pipe and supply other materials for street and highway construction. It is one of the largest firms of its type in the Midwest. In 1934 the Abel and Dobson companies formed a joint venture to construct the first public power and irrigation projects in the state at North Platte and Columbus, Nebraska. When George Abel died in 1937, P.J. Meehan became construction supervisor, a post he held until he retired in 1962, when he was succeeded by D.J. Costin. Other important officers were Morris Freshman, R.E. Eichelberger, and C.W. Hansen.

During World War II the firm did major defense projects in Nebraska, including paving at the Sidney, Mead, and Hastings ordnance plants and air bases in Lincoln, Grand Island, and Bruning. In 1946, shortly after George P. Abel, Jr., returned from World War II duty as an Army officer, the firm acquired the Reimers-Kaufman Concrete Products Company. In 1947 he was instrumental in organizing Universal Surety Company, and later Inland Insurance Company. Gene H. Tallman subsequently became president of the insurance companies and manager of the firm's banking interests.

More acquisitions followed, and in 1948 Abel Construction became Abel Investment Company, and subsequently NEBCO, Inc., which owns and operates the various subsidiaries and related family businesses. At the same time George Abel, Jr., and Meehan formed Constructors, Inc., which took over all construction operations. It is, and has been, one of Nebraska's largest contractors. It won the Mile-A-Day Award for concrete paving and constructed much of I-80 in Nebraska, along with major projects at Lincoln Air Force Base.

Later investments by the two companies included Concrete Industries, Inc., Western Brick and Supply, Nebraska Prestressed Concrete Co., Western Sand & Gravel Co., Nebraska City Ready Mixed, Nebraska Ash Company, NEBCO Cattle Company, NEBCO Intermodal, Inc., Ideal Concrete Products of Omaha, National Construction Co., Stewart Construction Co., and Kerford Limestone Co. of Weeping Water.

As the firms and their responsibilities to their city and state developed, NEBCO, Inc., and Constructors, Inc., made frequent donations to The Abel Foundation, which were used to support various institutions and charities. In 1940 the Abels made a substantial gift of Texaco stock to start the University of Nebraska Foundation and were recognized for their support of Nebraska Wesleyan University. Abel Hall at UNL is named for George Abel, as a reminder that the Abels helped build both Lincoln and the state.

George P. Abel, Sr. (1882-1937), through whose diligent efforts the foundation for NEBCO, Inc./Abel Construction Company was established. Abel Hall on the University of Nebraska-Lincoln campus is named in his honor.

DORSEY LABORATORIES

Dorsey Laboratories, the pharmaceutical firm with a nationwide reputation, was incorporated in 1908 by three traveling salesmen, William Smith, Thomas Dorsey, and William Widener, as the Smith-Dorsey Company. They opened a small shop on the corner of 10th and O streets, which has since become the site of the landmark Terminal Building, to distribute products manufactured by Upjohn, Parke-Davis, and Wampole.

Widener was somewhat of a "silent partner" from the beginning, and Smith and Dorsey, although good salesmen, had frequent personality clashes. Smith was a teetotaler, respected for his resourcefulness and reliability, while Dorsey "enjoyed a good time," and was known as something of a character. After only a year Dorsey sold his stock in the company that still bears his name. Smith, the only remaining salesman, was over-whelmed with work and in 1911 hired 19-year-old Richard Bennett, who became one of the major stockholders within a short time. He was a member of the board for 39 years and president of the firm for 16.

Soon Harry Prouty joined the company and the remaining founders left the business in 1913, after selling their stock to Bennett, Harry Prouty, and Harry's father, J.W. Prouty.

By 1916 sales totaled $33,000, and the firm built its own plant to manufacture its own products. Early in 1917 it bought 5,150 square feet of land at 233 South 10th Street, which was the firm's headquarters for more than four decades.

Sales more than doubled from $132,000 in 1925 to $276,000 in 1929, and the number of salespersons grew from 8 to 17. The number of products increased

dramatically, and the company gradually emerged as an ethical pharmaceutical manufacturer. However, some ideas went astray, like the project to extract estrogenic substances from pregnant mares' urine. At one point horses heading for the state fair whinnied, balked, and nearly destroyed the truck as it passed the plant.

Dorsey saw the need for more growth capital, and in 1950 it was sold to the Chicago-based Wander Company U.S.A. Sales volume rose to $12.5 million by 1967, buoyed by the introduction of Triaminic® Tablets, a pioneer in cold and cough therapy. The product strengthened Dorsey's reputation, and by April 1963 it opened a new 203,000-square-foot plant. In 1969 the firm was merged into Sandoz, Inc., a U.S. subsidiary of Sandoz, Ltd.

The year 1976 brought what was to be a significant change for Dorsey—the creation of an over-the-counter section. In 1979 the company changed its traditional "wholesale only" policy and began television advertising and consumer promotion. Today the firm

From its modern, 316,500-square-foot plant, Dorsey Laboratories manufactures and distributes pharmaceuticals nationwide, both to physicians and for over-the-counter sales.

Three traveling salesmen set up shop in 1908 at 10th and O streets, the site of the Terminal Building, to begin what is now Dorsey Laboratories.

continues to manufacture both prescription and over-the-counter products.

Its business is health. Dorsey employees have access to a company tennis court, softball diamond, and gymnasium, something Smith, Dorsey, and Widener had neither room nor time for when their business began.

Dorsey Laboratories' product lines, quality control, and equipment have continued to change with the times, thus ensuring a prosperous future for the firm.

LESTER ELECTRICAL OF NEBRASKA, INC.

Today's Lester Electrical of Nebraska, Inc., has a firm hold on its niche in the specialized battery-charger field for industrial and recreational equipment. Its products are distributed worldwide, through major suppliers, and much of the nation's industrial equipment owes its movement to the firm.

In 1963, when Cushman employee Lanny Carrier decided to leave the firm for which he had worked for many years, he had an idea, $10,000 in initial capital, and the hope that Cushman and others would see the worth of his new enterprise. They did, and the company experienced significant growth during its first 21 years, which was to set the stage for six successive plant expansions in the 1970s and 1980s.

The original Lester plant was in a brick building at 19th and P streets. The firm outgrew that facility by 1966 and moved to its present plant at 625 West A Street.

Originally Lester Equipment Company of Los Angeles, the firm grew really from the Lester Electrical branch in Lincoln, which Carrier founded. In the early days Carrier's former employer did most of the sheet-metal work for the charger cases, and Cushman was the firm's major customer, through its purchase of battery chargers for its golf cars.

But Carrier had no intention of remaining tied to one firm or one product. Within five years of its founding the corporation was selling to other companies, and had moved into producing components of battery-powered floor-scrubbing equipment. Today Cushman is out of the golf car business, but Lester Electrical still produces battery chargers for most other major golf car manufacturers.

The firm is still growing and Carrier does some of its sales work although he is semiretired and lives in Florida. Today the firm employs 135 people. The work force grew 20 percent from the fall of 1983 to the spring of 1984 alone. A new office wing was occupied in July 1984, bringing the plant space to 28,700 square feet.

That controlled growth plan has given Lester a specialized niche in the battery-charger market, under Carrier's son, Jim, the current president. The firm now produces 400 different models of chargers. Don Wilson, who headed the original Lester Equipment in California, is also semiretired but keeps an eye on the company's sales. Both he and Lanny Carrier remain on the board of directors. With marketing advice and a grant from the Small Business Administration, Lester has begun marketing its product in Europe, England, the Middle East, Japan, and Australia.

Lester ingenuity, and a sense of Lanny Carrier's willingness to take risks, led to the development of a patented electronic circuit that will help it capture 75 percent of all golf car charger sales, according to Jim Carrier, who has been with the company since 1964.

"We had some lean days," Carrier recalls, but the company has prospered and grown steadily since 1963. Golf cars still account for about half of the firm's charger business. "Regardless of economic conditions, people still play golf," Carrier says.

Contracts with several major battery manufacturers could double Lester Electrical's volume in three years, and the firm is considering moves into both the communications and the in-plant vehicle areas, which could prove again that Lanny Carrier's belief that an idea and the willingness to stick with it does, indeed, pay off.

Lester Electrical moved into this new plant at 625 West A Street in 1966, and has had several additions since that time.

LINCOLN PLATING COMPANY

In the 30-plus years since Dale and Joann LeBaron scraped together $3,000 to launch their plating business, probably no one year was more important than 1973.

The early 1970s were a time of change for both Lincoln and the country as a whole. A new environmental awareness brought strict new governmental standards for pollution control. At that point, many thought it would be the end of the plating industry.

Faced with the decision of whether to close the plant and throw away 21 years of hard work or go $1.5 million in debt, the LeBarons chose to move forward and build a new facility. When it was finished, Lincoln Plating had been furnished with almost $750,000 in pollution-control equipment. Today the company is termed the Midwest's leading metal-finishing firm and Nebraska's most recognized business for environmental protection.

Lincoln Plating Company began with just one employee in 1952, when Dale LeBaron purchased a small plating business at 2373 O Street. The company moved to 525 Garfield in 1956, and expanded there twice. LeBaron then leased another building at 123 North Third Street, before finally consolidating the facilities in 1977 at 600 West E Street. Expansion continued in 1984 when Lincoln Plating added another 16,000 square feet to the E Street plant, where the firm employs approximately 100 people.

Since its founding in 1952, Lincoln Plating has taken its share of chances and has usually come out ahead, and the LeBarons say it's because of the firm's ability to develop and keep talented people. What is often called the "midwestern work ethic" has paid off for Lincoln Plating. According to the LeBarons, their employees,

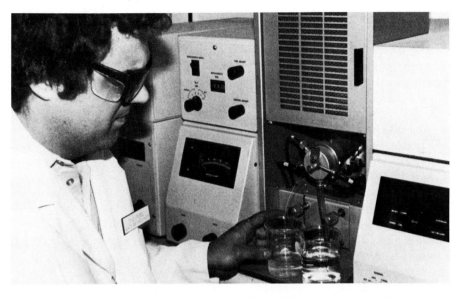

when given objectives, took on new responsibilities and learned to manage and to make important decisions.

The company has emphasized on-the-job and in-service training in an effort to constantly upgrade its work force. After work LPC people participate in metal-finishing classes organized and conducted by Lincoln Plating's own staff. Ultimately, the people pull together to help new people in the company achieve the same success.

The results have been significant. By working together, Lincoln Plating people have built a company that provides metal-finishing services to customers throughout the Midwest and to many of the nation's leading corporations in fields as diverse as agriculture and aerospace.

The year 1952 might not have seemed like the right time to begin a small plating firm. The postwar economy was booming, but some wondered how long prosperity would last. However, the LeBarons took the risk. As it turned out, Lincoln and its economic base grew along with the firm.

Today, despite its rapid growth, Lincoln Plating Company still holds

Lincoln Plating Company's quality-assurance manager constantly tests for trace impurities in plating solutions in the firm's technologically advanced facilities.

to a strong belief in the success of the individual, according to the LeBarons' son, Marc, now the president. The result is a team of people who believe in their responsibility to their customers and to the community in which they live.

The firm's 1984 work force has a variety of skills needed to manufacture products for a growing market.

BANKERS LIFE NEBRASKA

On April 6, 1887, just 20 years after Nebraska had been admitted to the Union, Bankers Life Insurance Company of Nebraska was founded by five Lincoln businessmen: E.E. Brown, J.R. Richards, L.C. Richards, O.P. Waters, and W.A. Lindy. Lindy was named the first president, and the first home office was set up in one room on the upper floor of the Richards Block, at 11th and O streets.

Three years later, after the Richards brothers disposed of their interests, D.W. Cook, Sr., John H. Ames, N.S. Harwood, and W.C. Wilson joined the company, and Harwood became president, serving until his death in 1900. Their leadership, and that of their successors, helped place Bankers Life Nebraska in the front ranks of life insurance companies.

By 1896 the firm had outgrown its one-room office and moved to the ground floor at 11th and N streets. W.C. Wilson assumed the presidency following Harwood's death in 1900, a post he held until his death in 1918. In 1911 Bankers Life moved into new offices at 14th and N streets, behind impressive Corinthian columns, which were to exemplify both the firm's strength and its continuing interest in the arts.

Howard Wilson, son of W.C.

The home office of Bankers Life Nebraska, at Cotner and O streets, stands on what was a cornfield only a few decades ago.

Wilson, was elected president in 1919, making him the youngest president of a U.S. life insurance company. He remained president for 40 years, until his death in 1958. In the late 1950s the company laid plans for its new home, to be built in a cornfield near Cotner and O streets, which it occupied in 1959.

George B. Cook, grandson of founder D.W. Cook, Sr., became president in March 1958, six days after Wilson's death. Cook's leadership moved Bankers Life from a regional to a national company. It reached its first billion dollars of insurance in force in 1962 and its second billion just seven years later. Under Cook's leadership Bankers Life decided to take another bold step and develop the Gateway Shopping Center on a site adjacent to the home office in 1960.

In 1969 Cook was elected

Imposing columns flanked the front entrance of Bankers Life Nebraska's downtown office. The building housed the firm from 1911 to 1959.

chairman of the board, and was succeeded as president by Harry P. Seward. Growth continued during the Seward years as Gateway expanded in 1971 and total insurance in force rose to three billion dollars. In 1977 Seward was elected chairman and Harold W. Booth became president. Neal E. Tyner was named Booth's successor in 1983, and Bankers Life reported over $4.5 billion of insurance in force as it met the challenge of a changing, expanding insurance market nationwide.

Bankers Life has always taken its role as a corporate citizen very seriously. From "staid and conservative" beginnings, it has emerged as an innovative and progressive company with 450 employees and a profound interest in the areas it serves. The firm has supported projects such as the nationally known Interstate Sculpture project, the artists in the schools program, and the University of Nebraska Foundation. This kind of community involvement reflects Bankers Life Nebraska's belief in a responsibility "not only to feed the body, but to feed the soul with creativity and beauty."

LINCOLN GENERAL HOSPITAL

Lincoln General Hospital has had a unique and close relationship with the city of Lincoln since shortly after the turn of the century, when residents had only just begun to dream of what a city could become.

When the Lincoln Hospital Association was incorporated in 1910, one of its primary purposes was to build, equip, and endow a hospital for the city of Lincoln. Stock was sold at one dollar per share, and a 33-member board was elected to implement the goals. By 1919 the Lincoln Hospital Association offered to contribute $100,000 toward the construction of a hospital if Lincoln voters approved a bond issue of an equal amount. The bond issue was passed, and plans to establish a hospital were formulated.

In 1920 the city council created a hospital board that was appointed by the mayor and approved by the council. The city would not truly own the facility, but the hospital, its property, and all of its equipment

were to be transferred to the city to be held in trust forever and used as a general city hospital.

In 1921 one of the city's most prominent residents, Robert E. Moore, died. His will bequeathed $100,000 to the Lincoln Hospital Association for construction of the hospital building to be known as the Emily J. Moore Annex, attached to the facility erected by the city. The will also created a trust fund for operating support. One condition was that the board members were to be appointed by the city council.

Construction at 2315 South 17th Street was completed in early 1925 at an estimated cost of $400,000. The hospital formally opened in March with 135 patients, not including 20 bassinets in the nursery. A hospital School of Nursing was organized shortly thereafter. In 1924 the John Teeters' trust fund (in memory of his wife) enabled the nursing school to erect a building, which was completed in 1928. Teeters and the

Moore estate continued to make significant contributions to the growth of the hospital during its early, formative years as more annexes were added.

By the late 1950s growth made problems evident and a decision was made to construct a new facility on the site. It opened in 1967 with a unique pod design that places patient rooms within 30 feet of the nurses' station. This feature was the result of a nationwide tour of hospitals by Paul Schorr, Jr., who was then chairman of the hospital's board of trustees. Today Lincoln General Hospital is financed by gifts, patient charges, and other funds without city revenue. But the ties to the city and its needs are still strong. Lincoln General created the state's first dedicated outpatient surgery unit and drew widespread attention for the creation of the Independence Center Chemical Dependency Treatment Unit for adults and youth. The hospital has become the trauma center for southeast Nebraska, and offers a 24-hour trauma transport team for emergency services.

Lincoln General also operates the region's only radiation oncology service for cancer treatment and a nationally recognized diagnostic and treatment center for sleep disorders. Full family-centered maternity and pediatric services are offered, as well as an employee assistance program (DIRECTIONS) to area businesses.

Many departments were improved and expanded in the 1980s to prepare Lincoln General for its second century of service as one of the finest community hospitals in the state of Nebraska.

The new Lincoln General Hospital, erected on the site of the original hospital at 2315 South 17th Street, opened in 1967. With a 24-hour trauma transport team for emergency services, the health-care facility has become the trauma center for southeast Nebraska.

LINCOLN CLINIC

When Drs. J. Stanley Welch and Edward W. Rowe formed a joint medical practice in 1908, Havelock was still a distant railroad town and College View was far down 48th Street. Six years later the young physicians became associated with Dr. Henry J. Lehnhoff, Sr., and they, as well as the city, began to reach out.

Group practice was a radical departure at the time, and the group that was to become the Lincoln Clinic in 1916 was one of the first in the nation to provide comprehensive care under one roof. The trio knew that the increasingly sophisticated field of medicine demanded more than just the traditional approach.

The organization's first location was in the former First National Bank building at 10th and O streets. It later became one of the first tenants in the skyscraper Stuart Building, on a floor specifically designed for the group. By that time, five other physicians had joined the clinic.

The city had begun to stretch out by 1956, when the organization opened a new facility at 3145 O Street. Shortly before the clinic moved to its new location, spot checks showed that between 5,500 and 6,000 patients were added to the records annually. By 1984 the number of patient visits had grown to 55,000 per year.

In 1972 another business reorganization occurred in which the existing partnership was dissolved and a professional corporation was formed. This move reflected the clinic's growth and its interest in attracting seasoned, committed professionals in a variety of health-care areas.

The Lincoln Clinic is a modern three-story, 28,000-square-foot structure located on a square-block area adjacent to the Woods Park Memorial Rose Garden, a city landmark. The lower level of the building houses a fully equipped radiology department, a comprehensive clinical laboratory, the physiotherapy department, and the medical records department. The top two floors are examination and treatment areas, almost identical in layout, with a large patient waiting room on each floor.

Right from the start, Lincoln Clinic has been staffed as a multispecialty group, with medical services provided in internal medicine, pediatrics, obstetrics and gynecology, orthopedic surgery, general surgery ophthalmology, and family practice. The physicians are served by an X-ray department, laboratory, physiotherapy department, and an optical dispensary. The building also houses a pharmacy.

From the unique three-room practice, the Lincoln Clinic has grown to a staff of 100 employees, including 17 physicians who share their expertise. The clinic is the largest in Lincoln and is the only multispecialty group in the city.

When they moved, the founders planned the new building so that additional floors may be added as the range of services expand. The Lincoln Clinic retains its original premise of providing complete health care for the entire family, in one facility, through an integrated, accessible approach to modern medicine.

The modern Lincoln Clinic building, located adjacent to the Woods Park Memorial Rose Garden, houses several medical specialties under one roof for complete patient care.

LINCOLN MUTUAL LIFE

The first home office of the Royal Highlanders, later Lincoln Mutual Life, was this Aurora, Nebraska, landmark, completed in 1905 for the young and growing society.

When the Lincoln Mutual Life home office building opened in 1973, in a park-like setting at South 27th Street and Old Cheney Road, it marked the end of one era and the beginning of another for the historic former fraternal order, now a major regional insurance company.

The Royal Highlanders was organized in Aurora, Nebraska, on August 11, 1896, as one of many fraternal societies at the turn of the century, which offered members "protection in time of necessity, assistance in distress, comfort in sorrow, and aid in the decline of old age"—in short, life insurance.

The Royal Highlanders' leading organizer was W.E. Sharp, an Aurora hardware dealer. The society opened its doors to 319 applicants, whose rituals and high ideals were to be based upon events in Scottish history. New chapters were called Castles, and were organized throughout Nebraska, Colorado, Wyoming, Montana, and Washington. Women's auxiliary members were called Fair Ladies, the

men, Clansmen.

By 1905 the Highlanders had several thousand members, including William Jennings Bryan, a member of the Holcomb Castle in Lincoln. The first home office was completed that year in Aurora to administer the growing operation. Expansion continued during the next two decades, and president Sharp moved the Royal Highlanders' home office to Lincoln. In 1927 he built the Sharp Building at 13th and N streets. The new facility was "a beautiful and commodious office and lodge room building," a Highlanders' publication said, "in the heart of the business center."

Longtime member Lewis E. Smith became president in the late 1930s. On May 4, 1937, the Royal Highlanders became a mutual legal reserve life insurance company, and was no longer a fraternal benefit society. It was named Lincoln Mutual Life Insurance Company on February 11, 1946.

After World War II returning servicemen became aware of the need for life insurance, and the firm continued to grow. In the early 1950s the company moved its home office to two floors in the Terminal Building at 10th and O streets until its present building was completed.

Smith was succeeded as president in 1954 by Grover K. Baumgartner. During the 1950s and 1960s a healthy national economy brought more changes in the marketing of life insurance, as well as greater rural sales.

John F. O'Neill assumed the presidency in 1965 and became chairman of the board in 1973. Introduction of new policies, more competitive interest assumptions, and improved mortality rates have been important factors in the steady growth of Lincoln Mutual Life, one of the nation's most financially sound life insurance companies of its size.

The company has a low-cost operation, partly because of strict budgeting and a sophisticated staff-developed computer system. It is licensed in 16 states and most active in the Midwest. From 1960 through 1980 total assets increased from $6.5 million to over $56 million. Insurance in force exceeded $600 million by 1983. The future looks bright for Lincoln Mutual Life, just as the Highlanders first envisioned in 1896.

The present home office of Lincoln Mutual Life, completed in 1973, looks out over the city from a park-like setting on a hill at South 27th Street and Old Cheney Road.

FIRST NATIONAL BANK & TRUST COMPANY OF LINCOLN

Today someone with a keen historical eye who looked down from the Nebraska Club atop First National Bank & Trust Company's 20-story headquarters building might envision Nebraska's capital city as it was in 1871, and see 48-year-old attorney Amasa Cobb pondering the future of this town of 3,000 from the door of the newly chartered First National Bank on the northwest corner of 10th and P streets.

A Civil War veteran and former three-term congressman from Wisconsin, Cobb immigrated to Lincoln in 1870. Impressed by the energetic citizens of the community and growth potential offered by Nebraska's virtually untapped agricultural resources, he immediately hung out his shingle. Shortly thereafter, with John F. Sudduth as cashier, he formed and became president of the private banking firm of Cobb & Sudduth.

With the Burlington & Missouri River Railroad rapidly expanding its lines from Lincoln throughout southern and western Nebraska, Cobb soon recognized that the resources of his private banking firm and those of a sole competitor were inadequate to foster economic growth for Lincoln and out-state Nebraska. So, on February 13, 1891, he called five of Lincoln's leading citizens together to prepare articles of incorporation for the establishment of First National Bank, and an application for a national bank charter.

The Comptroller of the Currency granted the charter on February 24, 1871. A month later, after Cobb had raised the $35,000 of paid-up capital necessary to launch the bank and changed the sign of his building from Cobb & Sudduth to First National Bank, the institution officially opened for business.

An active participant in Lincoln

developing into a mercantile, governmental, and educational center, and an important hub of the Burlington Railroad, First National experienced immediate success. By 1873 its needs for additional space dictated the building and occupancy of new quarters on the southeast corner of 10th and O streets.

Cobb's tenure as president of the bank ended in 1878, when he was appointed a member of the Nebraska Supreme Court.

From 1875 through 1890, the population of Nebraska and Lincoln soared and the economy flourished. The thousands of families that migrated to Nebraska's rich farmland were rewarded with bountiful crops and excellent prices. Employment opportunities in Lincoln found the population of the city reaching 55,000 by 1890. As a contributor to this growth by supplying financing to farmers and businesses, First National also prospered. Deposits totaled one million dollars in 1890, and capital accounts reached $575,000.

The golden years of the 1880s were followed by years in the 1890s in which mere survival was the major challenge. In 1891 First National absorbed the distressed Lincoln National Bank and its loan portfolio dominated by credits extended to purchase farms and other real estate at exorbitant prices. Then came the national financial panic of 1893 that coincided with the beginning of three successive years of crop failures in Nebraska, a resulting statewide outmigration of population that included the loss of one-quarter of Lincoln's 1890 census count, and the failure of five of Lincoln's eight banks.

In this environment, December 30, 1895, found First National in the

position where a depositors' run on the bank would have been disastrous. To quiet fears of depositors and lend credence to the stability of the bank, Charles E. Perkins, the highly respected president of the Burlington Railroad and holder of 100 shares of First National stock, was invited to become a member of the bank's board of directors. Perkins reluctantly accepted, knowing full well that if conditions worsened and other stockholders refused to do so, his conscience would dictate that he personally fulfill any of the bank's obligations to its depositors. The depression persisted into 1896 and 1897 and the institution's financial condition deteriorated further. Progressively, Perkins funded First National with one million dollars from his personal holdings and became the owner of all of the bank's 2,500 shares of stock.

By 1899 First National was again healthy and liquid. Perkins then sold all 2,500 shares of its stock for $362,500 to the state-chartered American Exchange Bank, one of

The original First National Bank building was located at 10th and P streets in 1871.

the three Lincoln banks that survived the mid-1890s. First National's name and national charter were adopted by the merged banks.

Although Lincoln's population did not again reach the 1890 census figure until 1920, the first 29 years of the 20th century were years of sound growth for both Lincoln and First National. During that period, deposits in the bank increased sevenfold and capital funds grew from $500,000 to $1.2 million. In 1911 the bank's building at 10th and O streets was demolished and replaced with a modern eight-story structure that was its home until 1960. During that period First National also acquired three distressed Lincoln banks—Columbia National in 1907, City National in 1923, and Central National in 1929.

Despite the impact of the stock market crash in 1929, the ensuing nationwide depression of the 1930s, and recurring drought that contributed to Nebraska farm income declining 57 percent during

that decade, First National remained financially strong throughout the period and, as recorded in 1940, actually experienced substantial deposit and capital growth.

The most recent four decades were marked by ever-accelerating growth by Lincoln and First National. In 1960 First National merged with Continental National Bank & Trust Company and moved to that bank's newly completed three-story building on the southeast corner of 12th and N streets. Four years later an adjacent eight-story addition was completed to accommodate First National's growing space requirements and to fill Lincoln's need for additional modern office space. Then, responding to the community's further needs for office space to

spur economic growth, the bank entered into an agreement with financier David Murdock to construct the 20-story bank-office building at 13th and M streets in which First National has been headquartered since 1970.

Throughout its history, it has been traditional for First National to constantly strive to serve the financial requirements of its customers with unparalleled excellence while also committing its financial and human resources to assuming a leadership role in contributing to the economic, educational, civic, and cultural development of the community and area it serves. Pledged to perpetuate this tradition, the management and staff of First National enthusiastically look forward to the opportunities to play a part in the continuing growth and development of Lincoln and Nebraska.

First National Bank's present building, at 13th and M streets, has been its headquarters since 1970.

First National Bank's second facility, at 10th and O streets, now the Lincoln Building, was the bank's headquarters from 1911 to 1960.

THE CLARK ENERSEN PARTNERS

It was late in 1945. World War II was over, and Ken Clark decided the time was right to leave his job with another architectural firm and set out on his own. His friend from Harvard, Larry Enersen, was just out of the Navy and needed a job. Clark convinced him that there was an important place for them in Nebraska, and the firm of Clark & Enersen began on February 1, 1946.

Lindale Subdivision, east of 48th, between A and C streets, was the new firm's first project. The well-designed, relatively inexpensive new homes were highlighted in the predecessor of *Progressive Architecture,* a national design magazine.

The 1947 recession slowed the economy, and Enersen was persuaded to move to North Carolina to teach. Clark stubbornly kept both the name and the partnership going, bringing Enersen and his family back to Lincoln every summer to pick up whatever work the firm had, mostly small residences and minor remodeling or additions.

One significant early project was master planning for the Nebraska state parks, which brought the firm recognition and laid the foundation for similar work for Chadron and Peru state colleges and the University of Nebraska's east campus. Then came the 600-unit Capehart housing project at the Lincoln Air Force Base and a 1,000-unit project at the Air Force Academy in Colorado.

In 1952 the firm began the second phase of its history by being selected to plan several Hastings schools. This led to more school work, and in the late 1950s and early 1960s more than 250 separate school projects were planned by the firm across the state.

The staff grew to 12 people. Bill Schlaebitz, who first joined the firm part-time in 1946, was there. Enersen returned full time in 1952, and that same year Albert Hamersky returned to Nebraska and joined the firm. After getting his master's degree from Massachusetts Institute of Technology, Hamersky had been on the design staff of Skidmore, Owings & Merrill in Chicago. The team concept, which the firm has nurtured, grew as Hamersky led the award-winning design staff, Schlaebitz supervised production, Enersen handled landscape design, and Clark continued to bring in the projects and serve as president.

By 1963 the firm had 60 staff members, including engineers and planners. Hamersky and Schlaebitz became full partners the next year, and a few years later the name was changed to Clark & Enersen, Hamersky, Schlaebitz, Burroughs & Thomsen. Harold Tarr was named an associate in 1964, and Charles Nelson was given the same position 10 years later.

The firm's nomenclature was changed again in 1977. The principals wanted a name that could last forever and reflect both the firm's heritage and the concern it had for the environment and for the opinions of both its clients and its staff. Thus, The Clark Enersen Partners was born.

Enersen retired in 1977, but remained active until his death in 1983. In June 1977 Hamersky became president and managing partner and Schlaebitz became vice-president. Clark retired from the organization he founded in 1979. Lowell Berg, Bernard Rempe, and Joanne McCandless were added as new associates in 1982.

The Clark Enersen Partners' work can be seen from Estes Park to Chicago, in churches, schools, office buildings, financial institutions, housing, libraries, and landscape designs such as the Foundation Garden in Lincoln. Its own NBC Center home as well as its projects reflect, according to Hamersky, "concern for the human environment and the emotional appeal of a building,—what it does to a person."

The Lincoln Center Building and adjoining gardens, designed by The Clark Enersen Partners, are a popular downtown recreation and concert location.

The College View Seventh-day Adventist Church, designed by The Clark Enersen Partners, has become a southeast Lincoln landmark adjacent to Union College.

ROPER AND SONS MORTUARY

The quiet dignity and serene surroundings that today are trademarks of Roper and Sons Mortuary might have seemed difficult to achieve in 1902 when Charles H. Roper entered the funeral business with Charles Beecher at 124 South 13th Street. This was a choice address as it was a point from which streetcars chartered for funerals, in the days before automotive processions began their journey down O Street's muddy paths to Wyuka Cemetery.

Still in its adolescence, Lincoln often was anything but dignified. It was testing its gradually developing strength as the capital city and just beginning to see its major institutions have a significant impact.

As the city tested new ideas and new boundaries, Roper and Beecher's new firm changed, as well. R.O. Castle purchased Beecher's interest in 1903. When Jack Matthews joined the firm, the corporate name became Castle, Roper & Matthews.

The pace had begun to speed up a bit by 1906, when Castle, Roper & Matthews introduced the first horse-drawn ambulance in Lincoln, long before the days when hospitals and then-independent services provided ambulances. The transition to the first motorized ambulance in 1912 was quick and somewhat creative; the structure was taken from one of the old horse-drawn vehicles. Horses have been completely retired, however, and the Ropers did have to scour Lancaster County to find teams to pull their horse-drawn ambulance and hearse in Lincoln's centennial parade.

From its beginnings, Roper and Sons Mortuary has evolved into today's modern facilities, and a fleet of hearses and limousines. Here, in 1905, a Castle, Roper and Matthews funeral coach is pulled by a team of black horses and guided by R.O. Castle (right).

The first modern mortuary in the city was built in 1911 at 1319 N Street and this facility functioned admirably until modern facilities were erected in 1960 on the site adjacent to Wyuka Cemetery.

The enterprise received recognition for its professionalism and care in 1919, when it was picked to become a member of National Selected Morticians. Castle died in 1921, and six years later Roper bought out Matthews' interest so his sons Reg and Max could join the staff. The firm further expanded its staff and services in the '50s and '60s. Continuity in the family-operated concern was guaranteed when Charles Roper joined it in the '50s and Bill Roper in the '60s.

Lincoln policemen on their "beats" may no longer drop in to make calls from the firm's phone, but the commitment to service to the community is still strong. This is reflected through the staff's involvement in community activities and its development in 1983 as the city's largest cremation service.

The Ropers have seen the area grow from a small prairie town to a thriving city, with expanding services and attractions, and the firm has grown and prospered with Lincoln. The long, chartered streetcar rides have been replaced by modern facilities, and a fleet of hearses, limousines, and other equipment helps Roper and Sons Mortuary provide the same care as when two eager partners first decided they liked the new town and the opportunity it provided. The horses and the muddy streets are gone, but the pride the Ropers shared as they grew with the city is still evident among the firm's 16 employees.

CUSHMAN
OMC LINCOLN

Cushman motor scooters put Americans on wheels for more than three decades. Then, as OMC Lincoln, a division of Outboard Marine Corporation, the company pioneered the development of motorized golf carts. Today OMC Lincoln is a front-runner in the design and manufacture of specialized vehicles for industrial use, for golf course and grounds-maintenance applications, and for professional turf care.

Cushman traces its history to the agricultural mechanization era at the turn of the century, and to America's fast-developing love for water sports.

Everett and Clinton Cushman, cousins, began building two-cycle farm engines in the basement of Everett's home at the northwest corner of 24th and O streets in 1901. With additional investors, and 100,000 shares of common stock valued at 75 cents a share, they built an engine factory at 21st and N streets in 1902. Cushman Motor Works, Inc., was in business. With five employees, the partners began building outboard engines for boat manufacturers.

Then, in 1909, Everett B. Sawyer acquired two-thirds of a new stock issue and assumed management, and the company entered a new era. Sawyer initiated development of a new four-cycle engine for potato diggers, grain binders, sprayers, and other farm uses. Cushman sold 1,000 of these new engines in 1910 and completed its first profitable year. The firm built a new foundry on 21st Street in 1913, which it still occupies. By 1922 Cushman had developed an air-cooled engine that eventually was used in a variety of applications, including lawn mowers.

The first Cushman motor scooter was introduced in 1936, with a special "Airborne" model dropped by parachute for troop transportation in World War II. The photo depicts a 1945 assembly line.

Then, in 1934, Cushman merged with John and Charles Ammon's Easy Manufacturing Company across the street. The Ammons took control of the company, but retained the better-known Cushman name.

When a youngster brought his homemade scooter to the plant in 1935, looking for spare parts for the old Cushman engine he had on the scooter, Charles Ammon instructed his son Robert to design and build a company-manufactured scooter. The first one was introduced in 1936. Almost overnight, Cushman motor scooters became popular. People rode them for pleasure and

A Cushman utility vehicle is used by security personnel at the Lincoln facility.

for business. They were used for delivery vehicles and mail distribution. A three-wheel version was used by ice cream vendors. Thousands were built for the armed forces in World War II, and a special "Airborne" model was dropped by parachute for ground transportation for airborne troops. By 1950 Cushman was turning out 10,000 scooters a year, and the three-horsepower economy model sold for $203.

It was also in 1950 that the firm pioneered the development of golf carts. Thousands were produced until 1975, when golf carts were phased out to make way for the increasingly sophisticated demands for specialized utility vehicles for golf course and grounds-maintenance purposes. The demand grew, too, for Cushman's line of industrial vehicles, and the U.S. automobile industry is still a primary user of Cushman industrial vehicles.

The company acquired the Ryan line of specialized turf-maintenance equipment in 1963, further broadening its marketing scope to the turf-care industry. The first riding aerator was introduced by OMC Lincoln in 1983.

Cushman Motor Works, Inc., was purchased by Outboard Marine Corporation in 1957, and became an operating division in 1962. Sales of company equipment have expanded to many countries of the world, along with increasing demand domestically for the Cushman and Ryan products. Herbert A. Jespersen was appointed division manager in 1974 and today oversees a work force of nearly 600, 10 percent of whom have been with the firm for 30 years or more.

Still located near downtown Lincoln, OMC Lincoln is proud of its heritage and confident of its future.

ALEXANDER & ALEXANDER, INC.

Until February 1971 Alexander & Alexander was a name not generally known among the members of Lincoln's business community. However, its predecessor organization, Weaver-Minier Company Ltd., had long been recognized as the leading general insurance agency and brokerage firm in Nebraska and the surrounding area.

On February 1, 1942, Arthur J. Weaver, Jr., and Andrew L. "Pat" Minier formed a partnership identified in the insurance industry as Weaver-Minier. They grew rapidly, adding highly qualified people—fire insurance rate and valuation engineers, safety engineers, boiler and machinery inspectors, aviation specialists, claims adjusters, and other skilled people performing the many complicated tasks inherent in the business.

Early in its history, Weaver-Minier became known to underwriters at Lloyd's of London for its highly specialized technical knowledge of utility risks and the detailed underwriting reports that accompanied every risk submission.

An Omaha office was opened to service business in that area and western Iowa in 1954. By 1960 the company was handling business for clients in 37 states and 3 Canadian provinces. Always, during its period of growth, Weaver-Minier adhered to its motto—"in pursuit of excellence."

The insurance department of the First Trust Company of Lincoln was purchased in 1961 and the officers and employees of that firm were added to the organization. The First Trust Company insurance facility

dated back to 1913 and included as clients many of Lincoln's oldest business organizations and families.

Just 10 years later, in 1971, the merger took place with Alexander & Alexander. The Lincoln firm of Weaver-Minier Company Ltd. and its associated ventures became part of an international concern primarily engaged in providing insurance brokerage and related services, human resource management services, and insurance underwriting.

A number of years ago Alexander & Alexander Services, Inc., became the world's second-largest insurance brokerage firm, with 82 offices in the United States and 49 international offices. It has 10,000 employees worldwide to service its many and varied clients.

In January 1976 Allen J. Mc-

Dowell became the managing vice-president of Alexander & Alexander-Lincoln. Under his capable direction, the company has continued to grow and expand its markets. The full-service office in Lincoln is staffed by more than 70 skilled specialists, consultants, and support personnel, and today Alexander & Alexander provides its clients with access to hundreds of insurance companies and specialty carriers of proven financial stability and integrity.

One of the cornerstones of this firm is its dedication to the community, the state of Nebraska, and the Midwest. All A&A people take part in the civic and cultural pursuits of their chosen home. Whatever is good for Lincoln and Nebraska is also good for Alexander & Alexander.

Alexander & Alexander's modern offices, now in the redeveloped Atrium in downtown Lincoln, handle a variety of related insurance services and loss-reduction efforts.

UNION INSURANCE COMPANY

In 1923 this Union Insurance fieldman posed in front of his new company car.

Union Insurance Company was only 37 years old when a smiling fieldman in rural Nebraska sent the firm's longtime president, James S. Farrell, a picture of himself alongside his shiny new black company car, with its official Union logo and a pet dog posed on the running board.

"Dear Jimmie," the fieldman wrote in 1923, "I believe my dog can lick yours. Come over and take a ride."

Some 75 years later, the company of which the fieldman was so proud and to which he felt so personally attached observed that there were then 32 insurance companies with home offices in Lincoln, and Union was the oldest of its kind.

As company cars changed and Union grew, from $171,793 in assets in 1899 to more than $56 million in the 1980s, the firm did not forget its early commitment to the individuals and small towns of Nebraska, Iowa, Colorado, Kansas, and South Dakota—its primary coverage area. In 1973 the firm became a subsidiary of W.R. Berkley Corporation of Greenwich, Connecticut, and a decade of significant growth began.

Further growth is projected for the firm, which began in September 1886 at Lexington, Nebraska, then known as Plum Creek. The Farmers Union Insurance Company was organized at a time when central Nebraska farmers were having difficulty purchasing insurance protection at any price from eastern companies. In 1889 the concern moved to Grand Island, and a few years later the home office was established in Lincoln. The Farrell family was the guiding force behind

Union Insurance Company for more than 50 years. James S. Farrell was a director in 1919. He became president in 1933 and served until 1942. His brother, Timothy Farrell, became a director in 1934, president in 1942, and chairman of the board in 1970.

Present officers include Robert G. Walters, chairman of the board and chief executive officer, who was president from 1975 to 1982 and has been associated with the company since 1949. Loren D. Graul became president and chief operating officer in 1982, after a long tenure with the firm. Other officers are Dean Fletcher, executive vice-president and chief administrative officer; Dale Graul, vice-president and secretary/treasurer; William Malone, senior vice-president/claims; and Harold

Dorssom, vice-president/marketing.

In 1962 Union Insurance Company moved from the headquarters it had occupied for nearly 40 years to a newly remodeled facility at 14th and Q streets in the former Mowbray Buick building. It had 75 employees then and grew to about 200 in the 1980s. As it neared its second century, the firm had 723 agencies and 3,400 agents.

Plum Creek, Lincoln, and Nebraska have all changed and expanded since the 1880s, and Union is looking to the future for increased commercial lines and regional growth. Its relatively new crop/hail unit now operates in 13 states, reflecting Union Insurance Company's personal commitment to both its staff and its clients.

The expanding Union Insurance Company opened a new home office in this remodeled auto agency in downtown Lincoln in 1962.

SAINT ELIZABETH COMMUNITY HEALTH CENTER

Saint Elizabeth Hospital, the first hospital in the then 30-year-old community of Lincoln was established in a converted residence at 11th and South streets by the Sisters of Saint Francis in 1889. Its progress since then has been closely interwoven with the growth of the city and of southeast Nebraska.

In 1891 a new, three-story brick structure was built to accommodate expanding services for the fledgling Saint Elizabeth Hospital.

In the 1960s a long-range plan was developed, which called for the relocation of Saint Elizabeth to north or east Lincoln, to better serve that growing area of the city with modern, efficient facilities.

Construction of Saint Elizabeth's new facilities on South 70th Street was completed in 1970. Today the health center provides 208 acute-care beds, and offers a full range of inpatient and outpatient services.

Saint Elizabeth has become a regional health-care resource to southeast Nebraska. The burn unit, which serves Nebraska and neighboring states, is recognized as one of the top five burn units in the nation. The neonatal intensive care unit provides specialized medical care for infants in a 17-county region. Both special care units utilize the latest medical technology and expertise. Saint Elizabeth also operates Lincoln's only kidney dialysis unit, where patients with kidney problems receive weekly treatments.

In addition to these specialized services, Saint Elizabeth is the primary family health resource in southeast Nebraska. Lamaze childbirth classes, parent education, and sibling tours at the health

Lincoln was 30 years old when the Sisters of Saint Francis established the first Saint Elizabeth Hospital in 1889 at 11th and South streets. A new, three-story structure (shown here in 1913) was built on the same site in 1891.

center help families get off to a better start, and a variety of birth options encourage family involvement in the birth experience. Saint Elizabeth meets the health needs of growing families with 24-hour emergency care, pediatric preadmission tours, pediatric intensive care, and outpatient surgery services.

Saint Elizabeth also has become a health education resource, helping people stay healthy. The Saint Elizabeth Wellness Center is the first hospital-based wellness program in Lincoln. Classes help participants determine their level of health and educate them to make better life-style choices. The Parcourse Fitness Circuit on the hospital's grounds provides a well-balanced fitness program that families can enjoy together, while the Sports Medicine Resource Center,

conducted by the physical therapy department, provides information, evaluation, and rehabilitation programs to high school and recreational athletes.

Saint Elizabeth also provides an array of management, information, professional, and support services to rural hospitals and other health-care providers. These services help ensure the viability of the health-care delivery system in southeast Nebraska.

As Saint Elizabeth grew with the rapidly changing health-care industry, it became a factor in Lincoln's economy. The Health Center is the city's 10th largest employer, with more than 1,000 employees. It purchases more than nine million dollars in supplies and services annually.

As it marks nearly a century of service in the 1980s, Saint Elizabeth Community Health Center is prepared to build even further on the foundation established by the Sisters of Saint Francis. The technology and sophistication of health care have changed, but the commitment and caring have not.

Today Saint Elizabeth Community Health Center is in this handsome facility at 555 South 70th Street. It has become a regional health-care resource to southeast Nebraska.

NEBRASKA WESLEYAN UNIVERSITY

Nebraska Wesleyan University opened its doors in September 1888 to 96 students and eight professors in the not-yet-finished building now known as "Old Main." Using ladders to get from floor to floor, they were the first citizens of an academic community resolved to be equal in quality to "any Methodist university in the United States," as the founders stated when the school incorporated three existing Methodist colleges.

Lincoln made the winning bid, and Nebraska Wesleyan University was built on the town's outskirts, surrounded by sunflowers and haystacks. An early catalog described the area as being "sufficiently near the large city for the convenience of trade, access to public libraries and privileges of the best musical and literary entertainments, and sufficiently remote to avoid the peculiar temptation and more expensive habits of the city."

The institution was ecumenical from the outset, stressing inquiry and the pursuit of knowledge that would build "genuine Christian character." By 1908, under the leadership of D.W.C. Huntington, Nebraska Wesleyan had 1,200 students in a college of liberal arts, conservatory of music, school of expression and oratory, teachers' college and normal school, academy, schools of art and commerce, and had an affiliation with the new Nebraska College of Medicine.

The school progressed in the 1920s under I.B. Schreckengast, but the Depression hurt programs, students, and the endowment, which was mainly in farmland. Given a choice between having their salaries cut in half or seeing half of their colleagues laid off, the faculty voted unanimously for the pay cut. Together the community weathered the Depression.

By 1937 graduate programs were

The Nebraska Wesleyan University class of 1896 and the campus they knew: the arch, the main building, and acres of prairie.

discontinued, and Nebraska Wesleyan became a liberal arts college. Benjamin F. Schwartz helped it survive the war years and later the school found new vitality under A. Leland Forrest. He died in 1957 and was succeeded as president by Vance D. Rogers, who, for 20 years, nurtured dramatic physical growth and rebuilding. John W. White, Jr., became president in 1977 and has directed many projects including the renovation of Old Main, energy conservation through computerization, and a reaffirmation of constituent support and the liberal arts tradition.

Today's board of governors oversees an institution that fulfills many of the dreams of its founders. Its more than 1,200 students are taught by a faculty, 75 percent of whom hold doctoral degrees. The student/faculty ratio is 13 to one. Nebraska Wesleyan's liberal arts

curriculum, revised in 1982, addresses students' personal and professional needs for the future, and the Wesleyan Institute for Lifelong Learning offers the same high-quality degree programs in the evening.

Nebraska Wesleyan University was ranked as one of the top 10 regional liberal arts colleges in the West and Midwest in a national survey of college presidents by *U.S. News & World Report.* As it prepared for its second century, the institution emphasized a liberal arts background for sound career preparation, thereby developing a well-rounded student who, like the institution, has a commitment to excellence and accomplishment in a growing community.

Dr. J.C. Jensen, a radio pioneer, taught at Nebraska Wesleyan University for 45 years. In 1921 he transmitted the first educational broadcast to Wayne State College. The photo, showing Jensen and students at the controls of WJAC on campus, appeared on the cover of The Wireless Age *magazine in September 1921.*

WOODS BROS. REALTY

After having developed real estate in Downer's Grove, Illinois, outside of Chicago, for Marshall Field, in 1876 Frederick M. Woods turned his eyes westward. Nebraska and Lincoln were the new frontier. With Mrs. Woods, two daughters, four sons, two cows, and one bull they arrived in the Prairie Town, intending to develop a new breed of stock that could endure the Nebraska winters. Later, Frederick Woods was given the title of "Colonel," and became the dean of livestock auctioneers.

In 1889 the colonel and three of his sons—Mark, George, and Frank—founded Woods Bros. Co. Responding to the needs of the prairie capital, they founded the telephone company, a streetcar line known as the "White Line," nurseries, and extensive real estate additions to serve the growing population.

During the boom period in the late 1890s the size of the area platted in Lincoln was approximately the same as it is today. Woods Bros.' first addition extended from Van Dorn south to Calvert and from 27th Street east to 31st. Farmers around Lincoln invested in the future also. Mark Woods sold these lots for $250 worth of a farmer's cattle and horses as a down payment, and took a note for the balance. This livestock was then shipped to Montana near the site of Custer's Last Stand, where the federal government provided food for the Indians in an attempt to keep them on the reservations.

Woods Bros. learned to move quickly from one opportunity to another. The company imported registered Percheron horses from France, Belgians from Belgium, and Shires and Clydes from Great Britain. Before World War I it was shipping registered stallions all over the United States, Canada, and Mexico.

The basis of Woods Bros. was always the land. The firm's real estate additions included portions of Havelock on the north, through the UNL east campus area, to the south and southeast portions of the city where the bulk of its work was centered. From A Street south, and from 17th Street east to 48th, a large portion of Lincoln was platted and developed by Woods Bros. Seeing the reluctance of citizens to move south of Van Dorn, Mark Woods built the present Lincoln Country Club to attract home owners.

Before joining his father, Mark, in the land-development business, Pace Woods, Sr., was in charge of their ranch and farm interests located in Montana, Nebraska, and Iowa. Later Pace Sr. manufactured the Arrow Sport airplane in Havelock. This was the first aircraft assembly line in the United States, and was established by him in 1929.

In addition to real estate and aviation, Woods Bros. also completed millions of dollars worth of work for the Army Corps of Engineers, primarily along the Missouri and Mississippi rivers and the Gulf Coast. The firm built railroad bridges, locks, dams, and sea walls.

In the late 1950s Pace Woods, Jr., returned to Lincoln from California, where he had been a network television director for NBC in Hollywood. Both Pace Sr. and Pace Jr. have kept their hand in land development, and Woods Bros. is now responsible for having developed nearly one-third of all the residential areas in Lincoln.

In 1889 Mark Woods made his first real estate sale to Charles G. Dawes, later Vice-President of the United States. Since that first sale 95 years ago, Woods Bros. Realty, under the management of Pace Woods, Jr., has become Lincoln's largest real estate company, with over 160 salespersons, 1,000 listings, and an annual sales volume of $150 million. Four generations of the Woods family have been instrumental in turning a frontier into one of America's most livable cities.

KOLN-TV/KGIN-TV

CORNHUSKER TELEVISION CORPORATION

It was a typical wintry day on February 18, 1953, when KOLN-TV, Channel 12, went on the air at 5:00 p.m. to become Lincoln's first televison station. Lincoln citizens had been viewing programs from two Omaha stations since 1948 but now they would have their own programs of local interest. In the spring, KFOR-TV, Channel 10, came on the air. In the fall of 1954 John Fetzer of Kalamazoo, Michigan, purchased KOLN-TV. The following spring he purchased KFOR-TV to obtain Channel 10, which was better for out-state coverage. When KOLN-TV moved to Channel 10, Fetzer donated Channel 12 and its equipment to the University of Nebraska, and Nebraska ETV was born.

Initially, KOLN-TV was associated with the DuMont Network and later joined ABC and CBS. Today channels 10 and 11 are affiliated with the CBS Televison Network, serving 60 counties in Nebraska and Kansas.

Since 1954 A. James Ebel has been the stations' guiding hand, serving today as president and general manager. John Fetzer is chairman, and Paul Jensen, who was there when it all began, is vice-president and station manager. Over the years viewers have come to know KOLN-TV's personalities as old friends.

Since its inception KOLN-TV developed strong local programming such as Nebraska basketball coverage, beginning with Jerry Bush in 1954; Nebraska football coverage, starting with Bill Jennings in 1957; the "Morning Show," which premiered in 1958; and "Romper Room," which began in 1964. High school sports have been a mainstay, too, with continuous annual

James Ebel (left), president and general manager of Cornhusker Television Corporation, looks over plans for the expansion of KOLN-TV's Lincoln studios with John E. Fetzer (right), owner.

Sportscaster Jeff Schmahl interviews University of Nebraska regent Ed Schwartzkopf during a special live pregame program prior to Nebraska's 1982 football clash with the University of Oklahoma.

coverage of the state high school basketball finals since March 1957.

In 1961 KGIN-TV, Channel 11, Grand Island, became a satellite station of KOLN-TV, broadcasting programs originating from both Lincoln and Grand Island. As KOLN-TV/KGIN-TV coverage expanded, so did its facilities and staff. New Lincoln studios were built in 1964 and its staff grew from the original 32 to 113. Beginning in 1965 translators in communities throughout Nebraska were built to spread the coverage of KOLN-TV/KGIN-TV. There are now 19 translators operating throughout the state carrying Channel 10 or Channel 11 signals.

KOLN-TV/KGIN-TV, with studios in Lincoln and Grand Island and through translator signal coverage from the northern to the southern border of Nebraska and as far west as Ogallala, has been a major force serving the state. Its news, weather, and sports programs are continuously rated among the top five stations in the United States, according to independent program-rating services.

KOLN-TV/KGIN-TV's current Lincoln studio facilities at 40th and W streets.

HYDROZO COATINGS COMPANY

Art Blackman loves bad weather.

"Wherever the weather is the worst, we do the best," the president of Hydrozo Coatings Company says of the international business that had its genesis at the turn of the century, during his grandfather Elmer's archaelogical digs in western Nebraska for the Nebraska State Historical Society.

Today Hydrozo markets the coatings it produces for building exteriors, parking surfaces, highways, and bridge decks in all 50 states and several foreign countries, backed by a growing research and development division in a modern plant near downtown Lincoln.

Elmer Blackman was in an excavation party for the Society when he discovered some Indian artifacts that were in perfect condition despite their age and dampness.

His son Jay, Art's father, recalled that Elmer spotted an unusual substance that had formed around the pots and protected them. Intrigued, Elmer brought the specimens back to Lincoln and began five years of chemical analysis.

In 1910, when he found the answer, he went to Kansas City to begin manufacturing the coating commercially. By 1916 he was doing major projects, including the old Hotel Bray. The next year Blackman treated the Commerce Trust building in Kansas City with the solution, which is still a proprietary formula. However, ingredients were hard to obtain during World War I, and the firm was dormant for a time.

In 1943 Hydrozo moved to a former brewery at 855 W Street in Lincoln. Jay Blackman had given up his position as the superintendent of the Gering schools to join the firm. Jay's son, Art, who had been working for another firm in St. Louis and also marketing Hydrozo

Elmer E. Blackman, founder of the Hydrozo Coatings Company.

coatings, returned to Lincoln to head the business in 1968. He then began an intensive marketing, research, and development effort.

Art Blackman targeted the East Coast and north-central regions as good markets because the weather there takes a toll on buildings. Hydrozo coatings protect Independence Hall and Congress Hall in Philadelphia, Pennsylvania; the Old Meeting House in Alexandria, Virginia; Dunbarton House in Washington, D.C.; the Mission of San Carlos in St. Augustine, Florida; and the Wright Brothers' Memorial Pylon at Kitty Hawk, North Carolina. In Lincoln the historic St. Paul Methodist Church also benefits from Elmer Blackman's "secret formula."

Arthur E. Blackman, Sr., president of Hydrozo Coatings Company.

Jay E. Blackman, son of the founder and father of the current president, joined the firm in the early 1940s.

As new markets opened and new products were developed, like a polymer coating to protect concrete from corrosion, the firm expanded rapidly. The coatings are also manufactured under license in Canada, and the first district sales office was opened in Columbus, Ohio, in 1975. This rapid growth meant more manufacturing space was needed, and in 1982 a new, 27,000-square-foot plant was opened at 1001 Y Street.

"You have to change with the times. You have to move ahead," Art Blackman says. Hydrozo Coatings Company is expanding its marketing staff and research division. He is proud that the firm is locally owned and controlled, with a commitment to community service and to keeping resources and expertise in Lincoln.

BRYAN MEMORIAL HOSPITAL

"Destiny is not a matter of chance, it is a matter of choice," William Jennings Bryan once wrote. "It is not a thing to be waited for, it is a thing to be achieved."

They hadn't conferred with "The Great Commoner" yet when a group of Methodist ministers and laymen met at Grace Methodist Church in November 1920 to declare that humanitarian and philanthropic motives "are the solid foundations on which all hospitals and similar institutions must be built." However, Bryan's philosophy of achieving destiny must certainly have been theirs when they decided to open a Methodist hospital in Lincoln, and purchased a site at 33rd and Randolph streets.

Bryan, who was to achieve national prominence as the 1896 Democratic presidential nominee and statesman, as well as through the Scopes trial, was prepared to move to Florida for health reasons when he learned of the plans for the new hospital from A.R. Talbot, his former law partner. The silver-tongued orator donated his mansion, Fairview, and 10 acres of land to the fledgling enterprise. The original site was sold to help finance construction, and the hospital's name was changed to Fairview Methodist Hospital.

Bryan died on July 25, 1925, and soon after the hospital board of

trustees voted to change the facility's name to Bryan Memorial Hospital, in recognition of his philanthropy. The Bryan philosophy of destiny and generosity wasn't forgotten and in the decades to come, the hospital, through the leadership of many, has evolved into a major regional medical center.

Bryan Memorial Hospital was dedicated on a rainy, blustery May afternoon in 1926. In 1929 the first school of nursing class was graduated. Today, as many hospitals close their nursing schools, Bryan continues to expand its commitment to modern nursing education through the Bryan Memorial Hospital School of Nursing. Other allied health professions are served also as Bryan facilities are used as a clinical site for students in a variety of disciplines.

Just as Bryan always seemed one step ahead of his time, the hospital, during its history, has kept up with the increasingly sophisticated and complex demand for the care of the sick and prevention of illnesses. By 1930 more than 4,000 patients had been served, and the first of many plans for expansion was initiated.

As the hospital has grown, so has its reputation in various specialties. The facility offers comprehensive cardiac care. A mobile heart team is on alert 24 hours a day to provide advance life-support services. The hospital has been a pioneer in the diagnosis and treatment of infant apnea, a condition linked to Sudden Infant Death Syndrome, and in 1981 was designated as a regional Apnea

Referral Center by the National SIDS Foundation in Washington, D.C.

The hospital's multidisciplined team approach to arthritis began in 1978 and was the first of its kind in the area. The facility serves area hospitals with mobile equipment units and analyzes computerized electrocardiogram readings sent from referral hospitals and physicians' offices via the telephone. The hospital also has a strong volunteer corps who help keep Bryan's philanthropic spirit alive.

In the shadow of Fairview, the growth continues. In 1982 construction began on the largest expansion/remodeling program in the hospital's history. The $58-million project includes adding 195,000 square feet to the main hospital building, space which will be used for support services, offices, and new areas of patient care and will include remodeling of existing hospital areas. Another part of the project, completed in 1983, includes a center for health education, an expanded school of nursing, and an energy plant.

William Jennings Bryan's mission—the need to reach out and help others, regardless of their condition—has become the destiny of Bryan Memorial Hospital, through the years a destiny of choice, a thing to be achieved.

Fairview, 1920. The home of William Jennings and Mary Bryan still stands just east of Bryan Memorial Hospital, which has become a major regional acute-care facility.

An artist's concept of the hospital as it will look following completion of construction in 1986.

BAHR VERMEER & HAECKER

Bahr Vermeer and Haecker, Architects', commitment to the creative use of space—old or new—is evident from Lincoln's tree- and kiosk-lined streets to the firm's own offices on the edge of the city's historic Haymarket district.

The firm's heart, as well as its home, is in downtown Lincoln. Formed originally by Deon Bahr and Robert Hanna in March 1968, Bahr Vermeer & Haecker began with three employees. It now has approximately 40 in its Lincoln and Omaha offices, and has pledged to help both cities grow.

"We definitely developed the philosophy that we wanted to stay downtown," principal Lynn Vermeer says. The firm took a former printshop and beer distributorship near the University of Nebraska College of Architecture, and turned it into corporate offices in 1973. A decade later Bahr Vermeer & Haecker had solidified its position as a developer of the downtown area, with an equally strong commitment to designing housing for the elderly and educational facilities, as well as providing quality architectural services to help keep small towns strong.

Vermeer joined the firm in 1969, and the partnership became known as Bahr Hanna Vermeer, Architects. George Haecker joined the firm in 1971 and the enterprise opened a modest Omaha office in the historic Omaha National Bank building, located downtown.

When Bahr Vermeer & Haecker opened its new quarters in Lincoln in 1973, the office was a visual statement to both the adaptive reuse and historic preservation of existing structures, as well as the interest in strengthening the central business core. Gary Bowen, also keenly interested in historic preservation, became a partner in 1976. Hanna left the firm in 1976. The following year Gary Goldstein brought to the organization new management skills and expertise in a variety of building types.

In 1980 the Omaha office moved to the Yellow Building, a 4-story, 100-year-old historic structure near the revitalized Central Park Mall.

With a diversified staff, selected consultants, and broad experience, Bahr Vermeer & Haecker's services span initial analysis through construction, design to architectural engineering, urban planning, and landscape architecture.

With impetus from a city administration and business owners who felt the downtown area must remain vital, the firm designed a downtown beautification project, which has won national recognition. The plan included the installation of comfortable benches, kiosks to provide information and color, fountains, bike racks, trees, and shrubs. The main intersection of 13th and O streets, paved with a brick sunburst, is now called Lincoln Center Plaza and is the home of many civic events.

In the 1980s the firm designed the renovation of a former department store into Gold's Galleria, housing shops, offices, restaurants, and other tenants, while retaining the historic integrity of the building.

The firm is known for its design of housing for the disadvantaged and elderly in Lincoln and throughout the state. Its Lincoln office is a convenient walkway between the University of Nebraska College of Architecture and downtown Lincoln, where Bahr Vermeer & Haecker has devoted its energies to the development of the city. The firm has won more than 25 design awards and citations from the American Institute of Architects, civic groups, and national and international publications.

Tree-lined streets, colorful kiosks, and benches are hallmarks of the O Street beautification project designed by Bahr Vermeer & Haecker, Architects.

Bahr Vermeer & Haecker demonstrated its commitment to the reuse of space in the downtown area when it converted a former beer distributorship to its offices in the 1970s.

UNIVERSITY OF NEBRASKA-LINCOLN

The spirit of newly gained statehood was still strong in 1869 when the Nebraska legislature chartered the state university at Lincoln. Two years later the University of Nebraska held its first classes in a three-story brick building on the outskirts of the growing capital. The institution was chartered under the terms of the Morrill Act of 1862 and committed to instruction in agriculture, the "mechanic arts," and military tactics, without neglecting the classics.

During its formative years the institution was beset by ideological conflicts, financial troubles, and a shortage of students, but it grew in quality and character.

By the mid-1880s the University of Nebraska had established the first graduate program west of the Mississippi River. In 1909 it was one of the first state universities selected for membership in the prestigious Association of American Universities.

Through the years many prominent graduates have had distinguished careers in the arts, business, and the professions. Notable alumni include authors Willa Cather and Mari Sandoz; Roscoe Pound, a former law dean at Nebraska and Harvard; entertainer Johnny Carson; and General John J.

Tree-lined malls dot the main campus of the University of Nebraska-Lincoln. Mueller Tower (rear), a landmark on campus, contains a 2.5-octave electronic bell, which is played on special occasions.

Love Library is the main facility of the University of Nebraska-Lincoln library system, with more than two million volumes and 21,000 periodicals, including special collections of the works of Mari Sandoz and Charles M. Russell.

Pershing, who once headed the university's ROTC unit.

Today the University of Nebraska-Lincoln has nearly 25,000 students, as the flagship in a three-campus university system. The campus is the intellectual and cultural center of the region and has a tripartite mission of teaching, research, and service.

Quality instruction is recognized in eight undergraduate colleges and in the professional College of Law. The Colleges of Agriculture, Architecture, Arts and Sciences, Business Administration, Engineering and Technology, Home Economics, Teachers College, and the School of Journalism offer more than 100 degree programs.

UNL stands at the forefront of discovery in many fields here and abroad. It has over 30 doctoral and 60 master's programs. Among

well-known research activities are projects involving mass spectrometry; cell biology; Great Plains Studies; transportation; the hearing impaired; Medieval and Renaissance studies; videodisc development; educational television, with a network among the four best in the nation; tractor testing; livestock and crop production; conservation; meats technology; animal and plant health; and agricultural marketing.

The university also reaches thousands through programs conducted by the Cooperative Extension Service and the Division of Continuing Studies. It has pioneered in the use of communications technology to aid teaching across the state and the nation.

The University of Nebraska-Lincoln's campus facilities are nationally acclaimed. The institution is home to the Sheldon Memorial Art Gallery and Sculpture Garden; the University of Nebraska State Museum, with its famed Elephant Hall; the Christlieb Collection of Western Art; the University Press; the Barkley Memorial Speech and Hearing Center; the nation's only tractor testing laboratory; one of the world's top atomic physics laboratories; and the Mass Spectrometry Center, one of six instrumentation sites designated by the National Science Foundation.

SELECTION RESEARCH, INC.

Dr. Donald O. Clifton, president, Selection Research, Inc.

A newcomer on the Lincoln business scene, Selection Research, Inc., is a modern version of the city's traditional union of education and business.

It started on the Lincoln campus of the University of Nebraska as a concept by a professor in educational psychology, Dr. Donald O. Clifton. Its aim, when the company was formed in 1968, was to identify talented people and place them in their most productive pursuits—fitting square pegs into square holes, as its logo depicts.

In just 15 years the firm has grown from three people to a staff of more than 200 full-time and 200 part-time employees. It has developed the identification and training of talent into a nationwide enterprise, serving such diverse organizations as the Boy Scouts of America. Xerox, Texas Instruments, Data Documents, Inc., Wang Laboratories, and Mutual of Omaha. Its operations have become international, with an office being established in England to serve clients such as a management firm dealing with more than 7,000 English pubs.

In its 15 years SRI also has broadened its scope of activities into public opinion surveying and the development of such diverse ventures as printing, banking, computer sales, and food service.

Some of its enterprises function as subsidiaries while one, SpanTel Corporation, has become a free-standing company whose stock is publicly traded. SpanTel, housed in the same building as SRI at 301 South 68th Street, is the creator of a national, and soon-to-be international, communications network featuring FM-radio-operated paging systems and the electronic transfer of data and messages.

From its Lincoln offices SRI telephone interviewers are in touch every day with persons all over the country to determine public trends and reactions on consumer and marketing issues, as well as public policy matters. From the results of these contacts, SRI has developed the AdWatch Report, published monthly by *Advertising Age.* This tracks the public awareness of various products being advertised nationally and is considered a significant factor in studying advertising effectiveness. Opinion surveying also is conducted for other national and regional clients.

A major part of the SRI activity continues to be in the identification and training of talent for a variety of professional positions, ranging from teachers and ministers to business executives and food-service operators. These services are currently used by more than 300 school districts over the United States and by a number of religious orders in selecting ministerial and lay leadership.

Using its own methods, SRI has attracted top talent to its key positions, including Connie Rath, vice-chairperson; James Sorensen, senior vice-president; Gary Hoeltke, senior vice-president and director of Research; James Kreiger, executive vice-president/treasurer; James Clifton, president of SRI Research Center, Inc.; Gale Muller, executive vice-president; JoAnn Miller, president of Human Resources for the Ministry; Mick Zangari, president of SRI Selection and Development, Inc., and senior analyst; Max Larsen, executive vice-president of Research; and Steven C. Fremarek, executive vice-president of SRI Selection & Development, Inc.

The Selection Research, Inc., headquarters is located at 301 South 68th Street.

AUSTIN REALTY, REALTORS®

Henry F. Austin may never have envisioned owning his own real estate business when he joined a local firm in 1938. However, when Henry's boss left Lincoln in December 1940 with the firm's bank account and the commission money from Austin's most recent farm sale, and left an overdue mortgage on the office equipment, Austin had to decide quickly about his future.

Neither he nor his wife, Edith, had the funds to maintain an office, but her father offered to help them out if things got rough. With a loan of $400, Austin Realty was established.

The Austins began with 32 management properties. Within a year, after finding more property to manage and handling rentals, they were over the rough spots. Austin was also interested in the development of the real estate industry in the growing city as a whole. He joined the Lincoln Real Estate Board and became its president in 1944. The following year he was elected president of the Nebraska Real Estate Association. He was also a charter member of the Lincoln Multiple Listing Exchange.

Following World War II home building began at a pace that encouraged the Austins to employ their first real estate salesman. With

Austin Realty's sales office and property management annex at 3910 South Street.

the war's end, an improving economy, and families needing homes, the real estate business looked promising. But Henry suffered a severe stroke in early 1948, and in June half of the business was sold. Austin died later that year.

Edith Austin continued to manage the business, closing the firm's downtown office in 1952 and for a time operating out of her home. In 1954 she formed the present corporation, Austin Realty Company, and new offices were opened downtown. In 1955 the firm moved into a small corner of its present building at 3910 South Street, which was then occupied by State Farm Insurance Company as its regional office.

Attracted by Lincoln's easterly growth, Edith and another associate purchased 234 acres for development between Vine and O streets, east of 66th Street. After selling her remaining portion of the undeveloped land in 1959, she redirected the firm's emphasis toward residential real estate. Mrs. Austin continued to manage the company until late 1964, when the business was sold.

On January 1, 1965, Gerald L. Schleich and a partner took over

the management of the business. One year later Schleich became the sole owner. He continued Henry Austin's interest in the real estate industry, being named president of the Lincoln Board of Realtors® in 1971 and president of the Nebraska Realtors® Association in 1976-1977. He was elected a director of the National Association of Realtors® in 1979.

In 1965 Austin Realty had five sales associates. Today it has more than 100. The company has developed over 25 residential subdivisions and provides a variety of services, including appraisals, new construction, and the sale of commercial and investment real estate. Austin also owns a title insurance company, a school of real estate, a property insurance agency, and manages over 1,400 properties, while still maintaining its residential emphasis.

Henry F. Austin (left) and his wife, Edith (right), founders of Austin Realty, Realtors®.

OLSON CONSTRUCTION COMPANY

When Charles Olson became old enough to leave his native Arvika, Sweden, for America, his father said to him, "Charles, there are three things I want you to remember.

"Always be fair and honest in your dealings. Stay away from the wild women. And never vote for a Democrat."

Olson followed his father's exhortations religiously, but later admitted that he had on occasion voted for a Democrat.

His father had a map of the United States on the wall of his home. The star in the middle of the map was to be his destination—Wahoo, Nebraska. Charles J. Olson, master stonemason, landed in Wahoo in the spring of 1882, suitcase in hand, with a bag of mason's tools, and 25 cents in his pocket, but full of ambition, determination, and hope for the future. Soon after his arrival he landed a job with the Union Pacific Railway, and was sent out on the main line to build masonry bridge abutments, an assignment which took him as far as the Great Salt Lake in the Utah Territory.

In 1883 Charles left the railroad to organize his own construction business as a masonry contractor in Lincoln. This enterprise was to evolve into a nationwide firm, operating in 22 states, with corporate offices in Lincoln and district offices in Salt Lake City (1941), Denver (1947), Phoenix (1970), Dallas (1973), San Diego (1965), and Menlo Park, California (1962). Olson Construction also has an associated firm located in San Diego.

Olson Construction Company was incorporated in 1914 with Charles Olson as president and treasurer, and C. Henry Meyer as vice-president and secretary.

Less than a year later the firm hired its first full-time, white-collar employee, John Hyer Miller, who began as a bookkeeper and rose to vice-president and secretary before his death in 1976. The new company bought its first concrete mixer in 1916. Charles Olson flinched when Miller proposed an additional purchase: a hand-crank

adding machine. That didn't make as much money as a mixer, Olson replied, but Miller got his adding machine—a used model—the following spring. Olson always kept his sense of careful workmanship with his eye on the books, but never lost his sense of humor or his Swedish accent. Minutes of a project negotiation meeting included Charley's remark, "Yust when I learn to say 'job' the government change them all to 'proyects.'"

The military buildup preceeding World War II sent Charles' son Carl to Ogden, Utah, in 1940 to oversee construction of the first 37-millimeter shell-loading plant to go into operation during the war. Carl was elected president of the company on November 27, 1945, six days after the death of his father. Under Carl Olson's direction, the firm began its westward expansion.

David C. Olson, Carl's oldest son, opened and managed the Menlo Park office until he succeeded his father as president and chief executive officer in 1975, when Carl became chairman. He spearheaded the Olson office network growth, with assistance from the Lincoln office's computer services.

According to *Engineering News Record* the firm Charles Olson started, with Swedish wit and tenacity, now ranks among the nation's largest construction and construction management firms. Despite its growth, Olson has not outgrown or discarded the basic value and tradition brought by Charles Olson from the old world to the new—hard work, a quality product, and unassailable integrity. Olson Construction Company continues to increase its market share in the Sun Belt of the South and Southwest.

Olson Construction Company has built more than 300 buildings in the city of Lincoln, a few of which are included in this montage.

LINCOLN EQUIPMENT COMPANY

The year was 1927. It was a long time before laser survey equipment, computerized welding systems, telemarketing, or Caterpillar D-10s that can literally move mountains.

It didn't seem like the most advantageous time to begin a heavy-equipment business in a state that was prematurely feeling the effects of an economic slump that would soon grip the nation.

That year, however, William B. Heilig chose to start the Lincoln Road Equipment Company, later named Lincoln Equipment Company, which would weather the Depression and even tougher times to become one of the nation's oldest Caterpillar dealers and a major supplier of a wide range of equipment.

Heilig, Don Bergquist, Sr., and C.C. McCracken were eager to develop their fledgling enterprise. In addition to an in-depth knowledge of their product, they nurtured a strong working relationship with their customers. As sales manager, Bergquist played a significant role in moving the company through the Depression.

The war years were a challenge. The firm focused on supplying machines and parts to construction companies building munitions depots in central and eastern Nebraska. Heilig died in 1943, and McCracken became president. He was succeeded in the early 1950s by Bergquist, who held the position until 1965.

After the war Lincoln Equipment grew rapidly in a booming period for the city. Early in 1947 the concern moved from its original headquarters, at 319 North Ninth Street, to a new facility at 930 West O Street. In the fall of 1950 Lincoln Equipment opened a new facility in Grand Island.

In 1965 Don Bergquist, Jr., became president. Under his leadership the company continued to be a leader in Caterpillar sales and service. When Bergquist died in 1976, his brother-in-law, Tom Larsen, moved his family from Phoenix, Arizona, to Lincoln to serve as president of the firm.

Larsen, a Lincoln native, was a graduate of the University of Nebraska-Lincoln and did graduate work there while also serving on the faculty. In 1959 he had joined Arizona's largest bank, Valley National Bank. He was assistant to the president and coordinator of marketing when he left the institution to found an educational, computer, and preschool business with a group of Stanford University professors.

When he returned to Lincoln to head the firm, Larsen spread the service and training philosophy he

Heavy-duty equipment such as the Caterpillar motor grader gave Lincoln Equipment founder Don Bergquist a head start toward the development of a major regional business force.

had developed as an educator and bank executive, and the Lincoln Equipment's expansion continued. In the late 1970s the company established new facilities in Kearney, Doniphan, and Omaha.

Lincoln Equipment's volume is approximately $30 million a year, and Larsen projects a 15-percent annual growth rate. From farm irrigation equipment to road equipment and other items, the inventory is becoming increasingly diverse and sophisticated as the needs of its wide range of customers change.

Today many factors, including technology, contribute to the company's success; but heading the list is people. Meeting new challenges, setting new goals, Lincoln Equipment people continue to use quality and service as their chief means of maintaining a standard of excellence for their customers that has been a Lincoln Equipment Company tradition for more than 50 years.

Lincoln Equipment Company as it appeared in 1950, when the firm began a major postwar expansion and added new lines and services.

MADONNA PROFESSIONAL CARE CENTER

The corner of 52nd and South streets has always been ahead of its time, a place for teaching and for healing.

Before the turn of the century, it was the location of Lincoln Normal University, which burned in 1898. Three years later Dr. Benjamin F. Bailey opened Green Gables Sanitorium, known throughout the region for its care, curative baths, and fine facilities as both a hospital and a teaching institution.

From its earliest years Dr. Bailey's top aide was Dr. May L. Flanagan, a pioneer physician and determined administrator who assumed the direction of Green Gables in 1944 after Dr. Bailey's death. Drs. Paul A. Royal and Samuel D. Miller were leading physicians at the institution. In 1958, when Green Gables was sold to the Benedictine Sisters of South Dakota, Dr. Flanagan said "the Benedictine Sisters usually accomplish what they start out to do. Mother Jerome liked the place the moment she saw it."

There was a little sadness, Dr. Flanagan said, but she remembered the people Green Gables had helped and those who had been trained there. "We had a pleasant home with good friends about us," she wrote in a farewell letter. "We had trees and sunshine and space." Mrs. Leon Hutto, secretary/treasurer of Bailey's Hospital, remembers her with fondness.

That description of places, people, and caring still applies at the Madonna Professional Care Center under chief executive officer Sister Phyllis Hunhoff, OSB.

In succeeding decades the institution developed into a full-range health care center for the elderly and disabled. In the 1980s it returned to one of Bailey's original functions, preparing professional personnel, through staff training and consultation to many other facilities in Nebraska and surrounding states. The teaching role of the historic site had come full circle.

In 1901 Dr. Benjamin F. Bailey opened Green Gables Sanitorium, known throughout the region for its care, curative baths, and fine facilities as both a hospital and a teaching institution.

In 1971 a new 132-bed building was constructed. By 1976 another facility was needed to replace the second original structure. A 22-bed stroke and brain injury hospital began operation three years later and became a recognized physical medicine and rehabilitation center for 17 counties. Madonna won the Innovation of the Year Award from the American Association of Homes for the Aged in 1980.

Services today include Madonna's Comprehensive Rehabilitation

Today the Madonna Professional Care Center provides programs to meet the spiritual, psychological, social, and physical needs of both inpatients and outpatients.

Hospital and Short-Term Restorative Care Unit with programs implemented for head trauma, stroke, orthopedic injuries, burn, arthritis, acute neurological diseases, and geriatric rehabilitation. In addition Madonna provides long-term care, support groups for the terminally ill, patient education, and adult day-care services. Mindful of the need for a holistic approach, the hospital provides programs to help in meeting the spiritual, psychological, social, as well as the physical needs of both inpatients and outpatients.

As Dr. May Flanagan said in her farewell letter, "God was very good to us all. We were able to help many who had no one else to rely upon." The tradition continues at the Madonna Professional Care Center, serving Christ's healing ministry.

CONTROL DATA CORPORATION

William Norris, the founder of Control Data Corporation, whom the Chicago *Sun-Times* once credited with helping create the computer age, hasn't forgotten what it was like growing up on a farm in Red Cloud, Nebraska.

"I always remember how much better it was in the small towns than in the cities," Norris told an interviewer. "You have an opportunity to find out the things you can do and the things you can't do."

It didn't take Norris and his company long to find out what they could do as the computer age blossomed. Norris believed in what the new technology could do for thousands, from Plato computer-based education system users in classrooms to business offices.

The employees in the Lincoln plant, who now number about 500, had to change as the computer age changed, from a business forms printing operation to a storage disc pack manufacturer.

The Lincoln plant has a long

history dating back to 1889 when the Nebraska Printing Company, later the Nebraska Salesbook Company, was formed. In 1959 the Victor Comptometer Corporation purchased the firm. The present plant, in the spacious South Industrial Park, was built in 1963, for Victor Business Forms. In 1968 Control Data, then 11 years old, purchased the facility.

Eleven years later the corporation announced the conversion to a magnetic media plant to manufacture storage disc packs for computers and rework existing disc packs for other firms throughout the world.

At the time of the conversion, the average employee had 15 years or more of seniority and had never worked in a computer-based industry before. The work force tripled during the first year.

As the computer industry grew, CDC grew also. There is a constant flow of technological change throughout the building, to which employees must adjust. CDC's Plato system, developed at the University of Illinois, is used by thousands for education and training. Control Data employees worldwide utilize Plato and other CDC-developed technology for training. The Lincoln plant is one of many such

Control Data's Lincoln plant is in the South Industrial Park.

manufacturing facilities, located throughout the nation, for the diverse Minneapolis-based corporation.

There have been many other "firsts" since the firm announced its first major computer system, fully transistorized, in 1958. The world's most powerful computer, the CDC 7600, was announced in 1968, and a year later the first Control Data Institute outside of the United States opened in Frankfurt, West Germany. In 1976 CDC began delivery of a new mass storage system and introduced Telemoney, an electronic funds-transfer service. In 1982 the company introduced its widest, deepest product line, CYBER 170 Series 800, the industry's largest array of software compatible system, at a worldwide users group meeting.

As Norris promised, he didn't forget his home state. In 1983 CDC gave the University of Nebraska $1.7 million worth of computer equipment to upgrade the school's academic and administrative computer use.

It is unpredictable to Control Data Corporation's management in Lincoln as to all of the innovative projects that may be on the drawing boards in future decades, but the onetime Nebraska Salesbook plant turned to computers seems eager to meet the challenge.

Even a major fire next door couldn't stop the Nebraska Printing Company, founded in 1889, from thriving and later becoming the Lincoln branch of the worldwide Control Data Corporation.

WESTERN PAPER-LINCOLN

For nearly a century, beginning with the Civil War until well into the 1950s, it seemed virtually impossible to publish a weekly newspaper in the United States without the preprinted pages, matrices, or stereotype plates produced by a newspaper supply company. Formed in that period to supply small newspapers (remember, personnel had been lost to the Civil War) and manufacture a quality product, Western Newspaper Union grew to become a dominant force in the industry from its national headquarters in Omaha. Readers were able, through the ready-print system to stereotype plates, to receive news of the nation and the world that most couldn't receive any other way. More features and ready-to-print plates followed, until mechanical advances and the closing of thousands of small weeklies forced abandonment of the syndicated service in 1950.

The Lincoln branch of the Western Paper Company formally began as the Lincoln Newspaper

Union in that period, and in 1884 was purchased by the Western Newspaper Union. John R. Hedge, who began work with the company in 1927 and became manager in 1935, was employed by the firm for more than 51 years. As business expanded a new plant was built in 1950 at 2005 Y Street (Western's present address), a site previously occupied by an iron foundry.

In 1961 the Western Newspaper Union Company was sold to Hammermill Paper Company, one of its major suppliers of paper. By 1971 more space was needed, so the warehouse roof was raised an additional 10 feet and a new section was added, nearly doubling the warehouse space, thereby making space for expanded lines of industrial papers, graphic arts supplies, and printing equipment.

There is the feel of a modern printing plant in the display area at Western Paper-Lincoln, for the product line has expanded with the industry. The firm still serves the southern half of Nebraska to the Colorado border and a good part of northern Kansas.

Hedge was and is "a hard-driving sort of fellow," according to current

This plaque honoring John Hedge was hung in Western Paper-Lincoln's entryway on the occasion of his retirement on December 31, 1976.

division vice-president and branch manager Gary Britain, and he, with a cadre of good employees, developed a market penetration for the company that is the envy of most similar-size organizations nationwide.

The firm is continuing that effort and philosophy of "extra service" that began in serving the small printers of its early days, still continues with many of them, and also encompasses the largest and most sophisticated plants in the area.

Western Paper has kept pace with the new developments in computerized typesetting, offset presses, and materials for printing reproduction across the broad spectrum of activities in the area. By early 1985 Western plans to step into a computerized warehousing and ordering system to link with major customers, suppliers, and paper mills. This will speed the flow of information and goods to its customers, who have long expected the latest and best from Western Paper-Lincoln.

Some of the 52 employees at Western Paper-Lincoln were on hand for this photograph, taken in July 1984.

UNION COLLEGE

It was a long streetcar ride from Lincoln to College View when Union College laid its cornerstone in 1890. Other cities had sought the new institutions, which Seventh-day Adventist leaders said must be a high-quality school with both a strong Christian commitment and a secure future. Lincoln made the successful bid, with help from business leaders who offered land for the new campus and welcomed church officials warmly to the capital city, which was just beginning to flex both its academic muscle and its pride.

Soon the clock tower became a landmark on South 48th Street (then College Avenue). The faculty and students proved to be industrious and devoted through difficult times. Their faith and community support sustained them as the campus grew.

Union opened a new administration and classroom building in the 1970s and named it for one of its pioneers, history professor and author Everett Dick, who had started the denomination's first Medical Cadet Corps. The clock tower, now a striking structure in front of the administration building, bound the college to the past and set its sights on the future just as the golden cords ceremony annually testifies to the worldwide missionary and service commitment of its students and faculty.

President Myrl Manley (1970-1980) knew that the institution must develop its faculty and facilities to better serve the ambitious graduates

The Everett N. Dick Administration Building, completed in 1975. Named for the college's distinguished research professor of American history, the structure houses three of the institution's divisions, classroom space, and an amphitheater.

of Adventist academies, while fulfilling its broader mission to the world. In 1976 he picked Dean Hubbard as his new academic dean and shared some of his dreams with the man who had been an official of Loma Linda University in California.

Named president in 1980, Dr. Hubbard brought to the office both enthusiasm and background in long-range planning, fostered by famed college and university planner Lewis Mayhew, former president of the American Association for Higher Education and a professor of Hubbard's at Stanford University.

Determined to remain at about 1,000 students so it could continue to offer personalized education, the school sought new ways to reach out to both the students and the community. It drew national attention in the 1980s when it put a computer terminal in every dormitory room linked to the college mainframe. The curriculum and staff were strengthened. Union expanded its campus radio station,

KUCV, into a fine arts community public radio station. The college music department formed new city-wide vocal and instrumental groups.

A new health center improved instruction and drew the city in for swimming and skating. Union began *Lincoln Magazine* in 1980 and invited more Lincoln residents to the campus for special events. A new library, atrium, and student center were built as well.

The commitment that opened Union in 1890 was reaffirmed as the college entered a demanding new technological age while retaining its traditional ties to individualized learning, service, and personal, spiritual, and intellectual growth. The golden cords would remain strong and were getting longer.

In 1983 Union College became the first liberal arts undergraduate school in the nation to place a computer terminal in every dorm room. These terminals will soon be connected to the Crandall Memorial Library card catalog, enabling students to access books and periodicals directly from their rooms.

PATRONS

The following individuals, companies, and organizations have made a valuable commitment to the quality of this publication. Windsor Publications and the Lincoln-Lancaster County Historical Society gratefully acknowledge their participation in *Lincoln: The Prairie Capital.*

Alexander & Alexander, Inc.*
Austin Realty, Realtors®*
Back to the Bible Broadcast*
Bahr Vermeer & Haecker*
Bankers Life Nebraska*
Bryan Memorial Hospital*
Champion International
    Corporation
The Clark Enersen Partners*
Control Data Corporation*
Cushman,
    OMC Lincoln*
Davis/Fenton/Stange/Darling,
    Architects/Engineers/Interior
    Designers*
Dorsey Laboratories*
First Federal Lincoln*
First National Bank & Trust
    Company of Lincoln*
Dr. and Mrs. Russell L. Gorthey
Hydrozo Coatings Company*
Knudsen, Berkheimer, Richardson &
    Endacott*
KOLN-TV/KGIN-TV
    Cornhusker Television
    Corporation*
Lester Electrical of Nebraska, Inc. *
Lincoln Clinic*
Lincoln Equipment Company*
Lincoln General Hospital*
Lincoln Mutual Life*
Lincoln Plating Company*
Lincoln Surgical Group, P. C.
Lincoln Telephone and Telegraph
    Company*
Lindsay Soft Water Co.
Madonna Professional Care Center*
Miller & Paine*
NEBCO, Inc. *
Nebraska Wesleyan University*
Nelson, Morris & Holdeman
Norden Laboratories*

Notifier Company*
Olson Construction Company*
Pure Water Inc.
Roper and Sons Mortuary*
Saint Elizabeth Community Health
    Center*
Security Mutual Life Nebraska*
Selection Research, Inc. *
Union College*
Union Insurance Company*
University of Nebraska-Lincoln*
Valentino's*
Weaver Potato Chips*
Western Paper-Lincoln*
Woodmen Accident and Life
    Company*
Woods Bros. Realty*

* Partners in Progress of *Lincoln: The Prairie Capital.* The histories of these companies and organizations appear in Chapter 7, beginning on page 135.

ACKNOWLEDGMENTS

As with any history text, scores of people answered questions and gave advice and opinions, but I especially want to acknowledge the help of Professor Wilbur Gaffney, who vetted the original manuscript through the eyes of a historian and an editor; Federal Judge Robert Van Pelt for discussing the Lincoln National Bank robbery and opening many of his files for my use; the reference staff of Bennet Martin Public Library and Heritage Room, and, of course, my wife Linda Hillegass and daughter Laura for their patience.

Picture researcher John Goecke would like to thank John Carter and his staff at the Nebraska State Historical Society photo archives and the library staff at the Lincoln Journal-Star Printing Company for their help in the preparation of this volume.

HONORARY ADVISORY COMMITTEE

William C. Smith
  First National Bank

Robert L. Hans
  National Bank of Commerce

George P. Abel
  NEBCO Inc.

Helen G. Boosalis
  Nebraska State Dept. on Aging

F. Pace Woods, Sr.
  Woods Brothers Companies

Earl T. Luff
  Lincoln Steel Division

Robert A. Dobson
  Dobson Brothers Construction

Richard W. Bailey
  Bailey, Lewis & Associates

SELECTED BIBLIOGRAPHY

Andreas, A.T. *History of the State of Nebraska*. Chicago, 1882.

Barrett, Jay Amos. *History and Government of Nebraska*. Lincoln, 1892.

Brown, Elinor L. *Architectural Wonder of the World* .... Ceresco, 1965.

Brown, E.P. and McConnell, Ray. *75 Years in the Prairie Capital*. Lincoln, 1955.

Chapman Brothers. *Portrait and Biographical Album of Lancaster County, Nebraska* .... Chicago, 1888.

Copple, Neale. *Tower on the Plains* .... Lincoln, 1959.

Creigh, Dorothy Weyer. *Nebraska: A Bicentennial History*. New York, 1977.

Curley, Edwin A. *Nebraska, Its Advantages, Resources and Drawbacks*. London, 1875.

Fitzpatrick, Lilian L. *Nebraska Place Names*. Lincoln, 1960.

Fowler, Charles F. *Building a Landmark: The Capitol of Nebraska*. n.p., 1981.

Gartner, Ruth E. *The Lincoln High School Story*. Lincoln, 1971.

Hale, Edward E. *Kansas and Nebraska* .... Boston, 1854.

Hayes, A.B. and Cox, S.D. *History of the City of Lincoln*. Lincoln, 1889.

Hillyer, Lois. *Lincoln Yearbook*. Lincoln, 1964, 1965, 1967.

Hitchcock, Henry Russell. "How Nebraska Acquired a State Capitol Like No Other," *A.I.A. Journal*. Washington, D.C., October 1976.

Jackman, Everett, E. *The Nebraska Methodist Story*. n.p., 1954.

Johnson, Harrison. *Johnson's History of Nebraska*. Omaha, 1880.

Junior League of Lincoln, Nebraska. *An Architectural Album*. Lincoln, 1979.

Knotts, Minnie Pres. *Nebraska Territorial Pioneers Association*. Lincoln, 1917.

Kolbert, Persijs and Jones, Carl. *A Survey of Historic, Architectural and Archeological Sites of the Eleven County Eastern Nebraska Urban Region*. Lincoln, 1971.

Lincoln City Directories. 1873-1964.

Link, J.T. *Origin of the Place Names of Nebraska*. n.p., 1933.

Longman, Anne. *Seeing Lincoln*. Lincoln, circa 1940.

McKee, James L. *The Wildcat Bank Notes, Scrip and Currencies of Nebraska Prior to 1900*. Lincoln, 1970.

————— and Duerschner, A.E. *Lincoln: A Photographic History*. Lincoln, 1976.

Manley, Robert N. *Centennial History of the University of Nebraska*. Lincoln, 1969.

Mattes, Merrill. *The Great Platte River Road* .... Lincoln, 1969.

Moomaw, Leon A. *History of Cotner University*. n.p., 1961.

Morton, J. Sterling and Watkins, Albert. *History of Nebraska*. Lincoln, 1913.

Nelson, Leonard R. *Nebraska's Memorial Capitol*. Lincoln, 1931.

Olson, James C. *History of Nebraska*. Lincoln, 1966.

Perkey, Elton. *Perkey's Nebraska Place Names*. Lincoln, 1982.

Railway Publishing. *The Capital City, Lincoln, Nebraska*. Lincoln, circa 1902.

Rees, David D. and Dick, Everett. *Union College: Fifty Years of Service*. Lincoln, 1941.

Sawyer, Andrew J. *Lincoln, The Capital City* ... Chicago, 1916.

Shaw, Lloyd. *The City of Lincoln and State of Nebraska*. n.p., circa 1890.

Sheldon, Addison Erwin. *History and Stories of Nebraska*. Chicago, 1913.

—————. *Nebraska: The Land and the People*. Chicago, 1931.

University of Nebraska College of Architecture. *Nebraska Capitol and Environs Plan*. Lincoln, 1975.

Wilber, C.D. *The Great Valleys and Prairies of Nebraska* .... Omaha, 1881.

Woodruff Press. *Beautiful Lincoln* .... Lincoln, circa 1911.

—————. *Lincoln: Nebraska's Capital City 1867-1923*. Lincoln, 1923.

Woolworth, James M. *Nebraska in 1857*. Omaha, 1857.

WPA. *Lincoln City Guide*. Lincoln, 1937.

—————. *Nebraska: A Guide to the Cornhusker State*. New York, 1939.

INDEX

This book was set in
Goudy and Helvetica Condensed types,
printed on
70-Pound Acid-Free Mead Offset Enamel
and bound by
Walsworth Publishing Company